'A wonderful read! A topic too often neglected and brought to light with drama, sensitivity and rigorous scholarship. Essential for a full understanding of the contemporary Jewish world.'

**Harry Freedman, author of *Shylock's Venice***


'*The Jewish pedlar* tells the riveting story of Jacob Harris, whose turbulent life became the stuff of legends and ballads. It also challenges any idea you may have had about what a Jew is or can be.'

**Miri Rubin, author of *Cities of Strangers***


'This innovative and readable history of crime is Kushner at his best. Weaving the seemingly smallest local detail into global historical themes, he offers an analysis that not only shines light on a marginalised personal and local history but explains how stories grow and change over time and place. Through Jacob Harris, Kushner brings to life the story of the Jewish pedlar, of Jewish/non-Jewish relations, and the history of racism and colonialism.'

**Gavin Schaffer, author of *An unorthodox history***


'Compelling, rewarding, filled with telling detail and provocative insight, *The Jewish pedlar* reveals an unexpected and adventurous story. A single notorious crime remembered across four centuries of ethnic and colonial history – Kushner's account ranges from obscure life story to transnational trade networks of diasporic experience.'

**Peter Leese, author of *Migrant Representations***


'The past *is* never dead. Unveiling layer upon layer, Tony Kushner makes this abundantly clear as he explains why the life and crimes of an eighteenth-century Jewish pedlar are worthy of contemplation. Beautifully written. A tour de force.'

**Milton Shain, author of *A Perfect Storm: Antisemitism in South Africa***

# The Jewish pedlar

Manchester University Press

# The Jewish pedlar

An untold criminal history

Tony Kushner

Manchester University Press

The right of Tony Kushner to be identified as the author of this work has been asserted in accordance with the Copyright, Designs and Patents Act 1988.

Published by Manchester University Press
Oxford Road, Manchester, M13 9PL
www.manchesteruniversitypress.co.uk

British Library Cataloguing-in-Publication Data
A catalogue record for this book is available from the British Library

ISBN 978 1 5261 7802 2 hardback

First published 2025

The publisher has no responsibility for the persistence or accuracy of URLs for any external or third-party internet websites referred to in this book, and does not guarantee that any content on such websites is, or will remain, accurate or appropriate.

EU authorised representative for GPSR:
Easy Access System Europe – Mustamäe tee 50, 10621 Tallinn, Estonia
gpsr.requests@easproject.com

Typeset
by Cheshire Typesetting Ltd, Cuddington, Cheshire

For Aimée and her county

# Contents

# Contents

Part I

# Evidence

# Introduction

Good people all I pray now lend an ear
Unto these lines which I shall declare.
A dreadful murder done at eventide.
In Ditchling just by the common side.

'The Ballad of Jacob Harris' (1734)[1]

This book is a quest in search of Jacob Harris, a Jewish pedlar and smuggler who went by many different names, ranging from the very foreign to the very English. As his aliases suggest, Jacob is a slippery character: everything we know about him relates to a vicious triple murder that he committed in 1734. His punishment was to be hanged and then 'hung in chains' – the gruesome process of gibbeting. The quest begins in a remote part of the English countryside in the early eighteenth century. But not all the answers will be found there, and we will have to travel beyond the obscure spot where the crime was committed to places all across the world. This will be a journey in time as well, from the early stages of modernity through to the present. The aim is twofold: first, to find out who Harris was and, second, to explain why his life and crimes are worth contemplating.

I want to rescue Jacob Harris, and other Jewish criminals, from what E. P. Thompson memorably called 'the enormous condescension of history'.[2] Harris does not fall within a heroic model of common struggle and resistance, and he was certainly no victim. But as a notable figure within a marginal community, he is more than worth bringing back to life. Indeed, as the only mass murderer in British Jewish history – except in the unlikely event that absolute proof can be found that Jack the Ripper was in fact an East European Jewish immigrant – he is a one-man illustration of Jewish independence of action.

3

My wider goal is to understand the reasons some Jews of pedlar origin committed crimes, including violent ones. I will explore both local and transnational
factors, especially the migratory origins of Jews and how, if at all, their minority
status was related to lawbreaking in the modern era. The book aims neither
to 'explain away' Jewish criminality nor to overstate its frequency. Instead, by
acknowledging its significance in complex societies in which the place of Jews
was fast-changing and uncertain, it will shed light on the wider Jewish experience from the seventeenth century onwards. And just as the Jewish experience
was fundamentally transnational, so too were attitudes and responses to Jews,
which helped to define the 'self' through the 'other', as well as the ambivalence
that was the norm in responding to both 'real' Jews and those of the imagination. Through the lives of Jews as pedlars and/or criminals and the wider construction of 'the Jew', we will see a complex pattern of the 'local' and the 'global'
interacting and constantly evolving.

How then to place Jacob Harris? On the surface, he seems a suitable case for
treatment under the heading of *micro-history*. The historian Peter Burke defines
this approach to the past through its various manifestations. At a broader level
it could be 'the study of the local or small-scale [a community, usually a village]
that is undertaken ... to illuminate larger problems', or of 'a biography of a relatively unimportant individual'. It might also be the 'narrative of a small-scale
event which may or may not have wider repercussions', especially collective
violence or the working out of factions and feuds. Death – especially through
murder – is a 'common theme', sometimes concerned with typicality and larger
cultural trends, and at others 'more or less for their own sake'. Many micro-
histories exploit 'trial records ... Indeed, a number of micro-histories focus on
the trials themselves.' All of this reflects a trend towards narrative, 'especially
"the sensational narrative"; the stories that victims or seducers produced about
themselves, the news reports, the adaptation of the original stories as novels,
and so on'. Unsurprisingly, 'micro-histories have a strong scent of sexuality and
scandal'.[3]

Aside from the last category, where there is only a little that will interest those
of a prurient nature, my study superficially fits neatly into Burke's definition of
micro-history and what he reproves as the turn away from 'grand themes'.[4] Its
setting is Ditchling, a village in mid-Sussex, and more specifically the remote
and largely unpopulated Ditchling Common, where the bloody triple murder
occurred. Legal documentation and newspaper reports, as well as later memory
work, including fiction, provide the backbone. Yet, rather than a case of 'guilty
as charged' micro-history, this book provides a chronological depth ranging

from the early modern era through to the twenty-first century, and a geographical compass that ultimately incorporates not only the British Isles but also the continent of Europe, the Americas, the Caribbean, the Middle East, China, Australia and Africa.

While Burke suggests that 'Community studies of the past appeal to nostalgia and to a concern for the survival of communities in the present', what follows is neither an easily palatable history nor one that is without violent disjuncture. Indeed, it hardly provides a reassuring version of the past, starting right from the grisly murders in 1734 themselves and the brutal punishment of the perpetrator. Where this study *does* conform more comfortably into the model of micro-history is its description as 'an essentially experimental genre of history. It is the kind of experiment that ventures something new and different; it is an experiment with no dependent variables.'[5]

## Biography, identity and the 'archive'

This book does not aim to provide a complete biographical account of Jacob Harris. Although the greatest effort will be made to imbue him with agency, there are simply not the sources available to create a full life story. Put bluntly, Harris does not speak one recorded word that survives in the many archives and record depositories that have been consulted. Only in the twentieth century has there been the imagination and a degree of empathy required in fictional work to ventriloquise for him. The task of the historian, especially of underrepresented and marginalised groups, is to find every hint of their existence. Nevertheless, however ingenious and energetic in locating these traces, there are times when the historian has simply to accept 'the limits of archive' – both formal and informal.[6]

Even so, there is no question – despite the events in 1734 now often being described as a 'legend' – that Jacob Harris *existed*. Moreover, that he was of Jewish origin is beyond any reasonable doubt. Indeed, it seems likely that Harris was the first Jew to be based in Sussex in the period after the readmission of the Jews to England during the 1650s. His pioneer role in this respect has its own significance, though there is a need for caution in making too much of this claim. As Giovanni Levi, one of the key figures in developing micro-history, warns, while 'historiography has ignored the working classes, women, oral cultures, everyday life, marginal worlds and societies different from our own ... it is not enough merely to mention a person in order to include him or her in the history of the world and show his or her presence and importance'. The 'crucial thing', adds Levi, is not the identification of the person but 'the mode of discussion', so that wider complexities and contexts can be explored.[7]

How Jacob Harris came to be in Sussex *is* significant: at the time of his crime there were no Jewish communities outside London, which was over fifty miles away, representing several days of uncomfortable travel on terrible roads. Indeed, how he ended up in Sussex and what he was doing there requires much more historical detective work than whether he was guilty of the crimes that ultimately led to his gibbeting. The reader expecting a story of miscarried justice will be disappointed, though the gothic grimness of Jacob Harris's punishment may still manage to shock and horrify.

In her remarkable recovery of the lives of ten Black Tudors, Miranda Kaufmann argues strongly that archives, rather than literary sources such as Shakespeare's *Othello*, must 'be consulted first'. She acknowledges that that archival material 'naturally comes with its own set of drawbacks and historical problems. The authors of England's parish registers, tax returns, household accounts, court records, and other administrative records did not set out to entertain the reader.'[8] Kaufmann's location and empathetic utilisation of these sources is exemplary, and they enable her sustained collective biography to be constructed. But even then, with the dryness of the archive, there is something missing in terms of recreating the lives of these African men and women. She meets that absence by starting each chapter with a short dramatised intervention that adds depth to each character and their contexts, providing nuances absent from the often two-dimensional archive.

Kaufmann's innovative and successful dramatic approach has not been used here – though I will incorporate and interrogate the various literary, artistic and cultural responses, as well as the local folklore, connected to the murders and their aftermath. Indeed, how the historian is to use folklore in the absence of other sources will be a methodological challenge that is essential to confront. How Harris was (re)represented, (re)imagined and (re)remembered from the moment of the crime through to the twenty-first century is explored in the following chapters as both their chronology and geography expands. The book will also explore the performative and narrative strategies of the more traditional archive, including apparently very mundane sources such as burial registers. Yet even if there had been an abundance of autobiographical/ biographical narratives, it would not *necessarily* have made it easier to get to grips with Jacob Harris and especially his 'inner', emotional life.[9]

Kaufmann's *Black Tudors* provides a collective biography that is broadly horizontal across its time frame, focusing largely on the sixteenth century. The focal point is the lives and contributions made in England, also embracing the transnational connections of those who were born in Africa or were second generation European. In partial contrast, my study constructs another loosely formed collective biography which runs across time and place to understand Jewish criminality and its association with peddling. It is a largely unacknowledged Jewish 'family' that Jacob Harris was very much part of.

Almost an exact contemporary to Jacob Harris was 'Jew Suss', a seminal figure in Jewish/non-Jewish relations in early modern Germany whose distorted memory became central in the history of antisemitism. Yair Mintzker has studied 'Jew Suss', and even with the advantage of a wealth of contemporary accounts – trial records, full length 'instant' biographies and later extensive memory work – he argues that 'The historical figure of Joseph Suss Oppenheimer is incredibly elusive.' Unlike Jacob Harris, Oppenheimer was found guilty in 1738 of a crime he did not commit. Indeed, it was never clear what 'Jew Suss' was alleged to have done, so great was the prejudice against him and his Jewishness. We will return to the parallels – two Jews of German origin who were hanged and gibbeted within a few years of each other in different parts of Europe. How was it that one figure became notorious in the development of Jew hatred in Germany while the other was relegated to a footnote (and even then at a later stage) in the history of antisemitism in the United Kingdom? Here it suffices to note that even with more contemporary documentation about him, it would still not be easy – if indeed possible – to find the 'real' Jacob Harris and to recreate his ambitions, fears, loyalties and wider world view.

As Mintzker suggests, with the trial records, 'there is hardly a narrative about Oppenheimer one could *not* support with some documentation. Finding out the truth in this case, though a noble endeavour, proves much harder in practice than in theory.'[10] In the case of Jacob Harris we are at a further disadvantage. Although there are extensive contemporary accounts of his crime before and after he was caught, the trial itself produced a legal record that stated in essence only that he was guilty. Contemporary newspaper reports of the trial, which probably lasted only a matter of minutes, offer little more. The archive record is rich and varied and can, with care, be teased out further. At no point, however, is anything approaching a biography of Jacob Harris provided in that record. There is a strong hint of a close relative in an archive collection unrelated to the murders, but beyond that we do not know anything directly about his family background. Those tried at the Old Bailey and executed in London had their life story written and sold by the 'Ordinary', the chaplain who was responsible for them during their stay in Newgate prison. Such sources – not that dissimilar to those relating to 'Jew Suss' – present many challenges, but they do provide

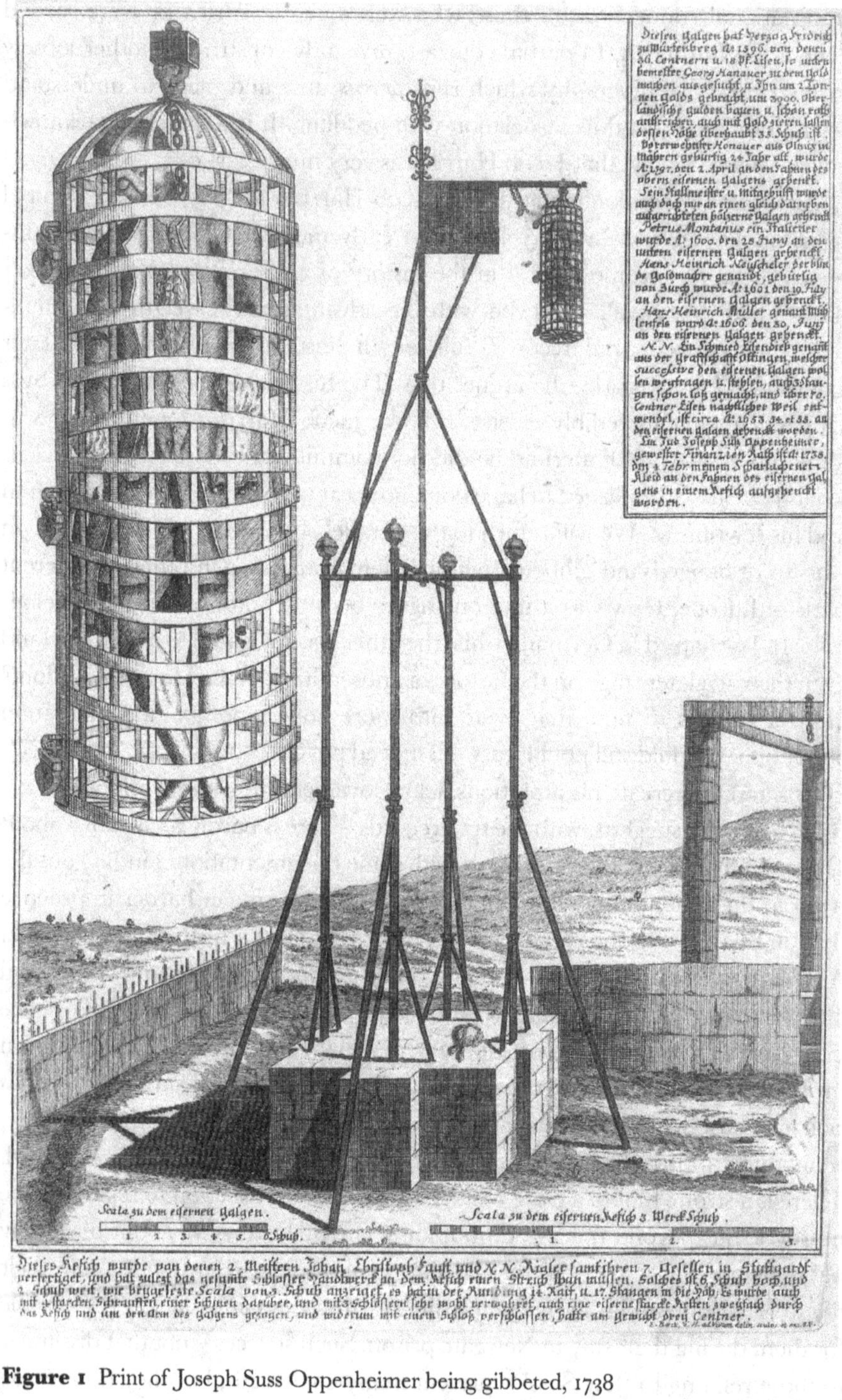

**Figure 1** Print of Joseph Suss Oppenheimer being gibbeted, 1738

evidence at least of family background. However, being tried in Horsham, forty miles from London, meant that Harris did not receive such extensive attention.

Aside from the role of chance in what does and does not survive in the archive, this study takes the general stance that there are 'no innocent deposits': what is included in formal repositories reflects wider societal attitudes and power relationships, especially the politics of inclusion and exclusion.[11] Archives are, indeed, 'privileged sites'.[12] A frustrating loss is the original broadside, *The Ballad of Jacob Harris*, which would have been mass produced in the summer of 1734. It described the murders in Ditchling Common in some (gory) detail. Thousands of other cheap and widely consumed contemporary ballads *have* survived and form the basis of huge international, digitised archives. On the one hand, the loss of the original of *The Ballad of Jacob Harris* is just misfortune. On the other, it reflects the snobberies of those collecting such broadsides as well as the remoteness of Ditchling and its Common – even in the nineteenth century, when the folk collectors were at their most active, extensively so in Sussex.

*The Ballad of Jacob Harris* was discovered by county antiquarians a century after the murders took place, but it was ridiculed for its 'very rude [that is unsophisticated] verses'. They did not consider it important enough to keep it in their collections, which formed the basis for later local record offices in Sussex.[13] Later versions *have* survived and they are similar to each other but differ in critical matters – especially the background of the murderer. Finding the original broadside, however, has proved elusive, and the subtle variations that were later published tell us as much about those reproducing them as those that, in haste, put it together and sold it at the time of Harris's gibbeting. Throughout this study, it will thus be crucial to explore the nature of the broadly defined 'archive', which in this case includes more traditional records alongside material culture, autobiography, music, art and the landscape. I will consider how the archive was constructed, what it excluded and what access it allows us to the world of Jacob Harris and of other pedlars in different times and places.

As a history from below, this study explores the lives of ordinary people, and autobiographical practice is to the fore. It is not enough, however, to simply quote from such sources to recover lost or marginal voices and experiences. First, as Mary Chamberlain and Paul Thompson insist, 'Any life story ... is shaped not only by the re-workings of experience through memory and re-evaluation but always ... through art.'[14] Second, and linked, in the case of the focal points of this study – peddling and criminality – narrative expectations and the power of collective memory often help shape the texts we will be encountering – including silences within them. Regarding the Jewish pedlar, for example, it has been noted how individual as well as communal histories tend to be celebratory, with expectations of economic success and integration.[15] Third, there is the conundrum famously posed by Gayatri Chakravorty Spivak: 'Can the subaltern speak?' In the case of sacrificed widows, she is pessimistic about the relevant court records in the East India Company: 'one cannot put together a "voice"', concluding that 'if you are poor, black, and female you get it in three ways'.[16]

Here, while the context is largely within the British Empire, the people studied were not colonial subjects and they were mainly male. Nevertheless, their ethno-religious and economic marginality, as well as their legal and later racialised status, must be considered and we should raise the question: what are the autobiographical writings of Jewish pedlars and/or criminals *for*? In short, they should not be taken at face value and quoted merely to provide local colour. Again, the archive must not be treated as a given, especially as we are lucky that it is relatively rich in examples of life story. There are Jewish pedlar accounts from as early as the eighteenth century and forms of oral testimony from when Henry Mayhew published an interview with a Moroccan Jewish pedlar as part of his classic *London Labour and the London Poor* in the mid-nineteenth century. Mayhew reproduced a remarkable life story of a man who said he had been 'smuggled' into Gibraltar and from there eventually to selling rhubarb on the streets of the capital of the UK.[17] The accounts by the prison Ordinaries of about-to-be executed criminals have been mentioned. As with the pedlar life stories, the accounts relating to Jewish criminals are rich sources, but they need to be treated very cautiously if we are to consider whether the Jewish villain can 'speak' – so strong is the Ordinaries' moral abhorrence and sensational content.

The biographical focus of this study uses Jacob Harris as its starting point; the other individuals covered have two key aspects in common. First, they defined themselves or were defined by others as Jewish. Second, careerwise they were pedlars and/or criminals. These particular – and, on the surface, peculiar – prisms require some justification. In his provocative *How Jewish is Jewish History?* (2007), Moshe Rosman critiqued what he saw as a new generation of 'academic experts in Jewish studies [who] have tended to disparage the investigation of "the Jewish contribution to civilization"' approach of earlier scholars. The new scholars write from the premise that 'Jews … no [longer] need to prove their worthiness'. Rosman adds, 'As if to drive this home, many … revel in a new-found capacity to parade Jewish foibles, misdeeds, and mistreatment of others … Convinced that skeletons in the Jewish collective closet will not be held against them.'[18]

Such challenging scholarship has itself led to a defensive reaction.[19] Todd Endelman, whose seminal work during the 1970s and beyond on the Jews of Georgian England helped provide the foundation for this study, recalls how a 'notable of the Jewish Historical Society of England ... claimed ... that I was preoccupied with Jewish vagabonds and criminals'. It was a criticism hardly representative of Endelman's writing: it would seem that even a little was too much 'dirt'.[20] More recently, Ephraim Shoham-Steiner, author of a path-breaking study of Jews and crime in medieval Europe, was advised strongly by his colleagues at Ben-Gurion University in Israel 'not to pursue the subject', lest it give ammunition to antisemites.[21] What is intended here, following Endelman and Shoham-Steiner, is neither polemic nor apologetics. Instead, the aim is to provide a contextualised Jewish history based extensively on the study of individuals on the margins of society, covering the period from the early modern to the post-Holocaust era. It is a social and cultural history of ordinary, rarely prominent Jews, and is thus part of the history from below movement that emerged from the 1960s, emphasising especially the importance of the 'everyday'.

If it is a form of recovery history, it is not in the celebratory mode – certainly not for the criminals studied, whose violence and actions were abhorrent. The dangers of a triumphal history are even greater for the Jewish pedlars, who have been given a largely uncritical treatment in the worlds of history and heritage. Despite their ordinariness, these pedlars and criminals (and those such as Jacob Harris, who crossed over between the two) led remarkable if often disturbing lives. They shed light not only on the wider Jewish experience in the modern era (Endelman in his defence of Jewish social history highlights that it was more philosophers such as Moses Mendelssohn who were 'atypical and marginal' than the mass of ordinary Jews),[22] but also on the wider field of Jewish/non-Jewish relations from the eighteenth century onwards.

Some technical and historiographical clarification is in order with the categories of both ethno-religious identity and occupation. With regard to Jewishness, sources such as names are often a good guide, reflecting specific conventions and histories, even if these are not always definitive. For example, biblical names in the British context might reflect wider identification with the Old Testament, especially within Christian nonconformity. There may also be acculturation in Jewish naming where this was legally permitted. In large-scale quantitative samples occasional misidentifications do not matter in identifying the Jewish presence in a locality. But in terms of the individual, Jewishness is far more complicated. She/he may have a fluidity in terms of self-identification which might go beyond a simplistic Jewish/non-Jewish binary. More commonly individuals may regard their Jewishness as only one of many – and not necessarily the most important – of their often-competing identities, which are further complicated by shifts in focus over the life cycle. They may, or may not, be regarded as Jewish by the outside world and within the organised Jewish community. Mayhew's pedlar, for example, claimed he could not attend the Jewish hospital in London because his second wife was Christian.[23]

To add further layers of complexity, the Jewish world has never been free of conflict, whether religious, cultural, economic or political. Tensions between settled Jews and those of recent migrant origin will become particularly clear in this study. In her *Masculinity and the Making of American Judaism* (2017), Sarah Imhoff is at pains to emphasise from the start that 'there is no Jewish experience, or identity, in the singular'.[24] Scholars thus need to be careful not to impose an identity which might have been unimportant or even alien to those they are studying. The case of Jacob Harris is especially tricky, with the evidence that survives: the dangers of leaping to conclusions will be kept in mind throughout. For later commentators, Jacob Harris's Jewishness, negatively construed, was critical to understanding him and especially why he committed the murders. That was not, however, a widespread contemporary perspective on him in the 1730s – as far as the broadly defined archive will permit us to judge.

In terms of occupation, let us turn first to peddling, which was a common – if not *the most* common – occupation of Jews from the eighteenth to the late nineteenth centuries, around the world. Peddling was often a temporary occupation for Jews – one that might be returned to at different times during the work life cycle, especially when other opportunities were in short supply. That was certainly true of Mayhew's Moroccan Jewish rhubarb seller, who started as a pedlar in Britain and then returned to peddling later in life after his West Country business failed.[25] For others, peddling was their only occupation and the rigours of that way of life sometimes led to ill health and early death. It is remarkable that despite its importance in Jewish economic history, peddling has an extremely limited historiography and muted presence in the world of Jewish heritage in the form of museums and displays. What there is, however, has a strong underlying narrative of upward economic progression. Figures such as Levi Strauss in America, Sammy Marks in South Africa and Henry Moses in England are to the fore. In what is the only full-length study of Jewish pedlars in the modern world, focusing especially on their impact in the 'New World', Hasia Diner concludes with a poetic love letter to their achievements and the benefits brought to their customers:

the woman in provincial England in the late eighteenth century who had never before owned eyeglasses saw the world differently after the immigrant Jewish peddler pulled a pair from his sack. The poor people of Colombia who had owned no shoes until the immigrant peddlers arrived, afterward felt the ground beneath their feet far differently, and less painfully ... Women around the new world who spread sheets and pillowcases on their beds, adorned their walls with mirrors, pictures and picture frames, bought from the peddlers and thus lived more comfortably and with an altered aesthetic.

From this, argues Diner, the non-Jewish world became more familiar and empathetic towards Jews, regarding them as 'real human beings'. In turn, the Jewish pedlars became merchants and respectable citizens, and their children 'went into the teaching profession, politics, social reform movements, social work, law, medicine, the academy, entertainment, literature, and the arts'.[26]

Several generations earlier, Cecil Roth, who might be called the founder of Jewish pedlar studies, confined his 1930s research to the eighteenth century in England, but his general conclusions predicted those of Diner. In an article initially and revealingly entitled 'Antecedents of Aristocracy', Roth praised the pioneer role of the Jewish pedlar in founding provincial communities in England, suggesting that by the accession of Queen Victoria they had 'gradually died out, or else amassed sufficient property to set up shop'. He playfully concluded, going even further than Diner later dared, that the pedlars' descendants 'preside over board meetings in the City and over dinner tables in Mayfair'.[27]

What follows is an alternative model to those of Roth and Diner: not belittling the courage and determination of the Jewish pedlar (and following the remarkable global optic of the latter scholar), but suggesting that the large majority were far from 'rags to riches' stories. Moreover, Jewish/non-Jewish relations through the prism of the pedlar were complex and not always positive.[28] Chronologically, the story certainly does not end with the passing of the Georgian era, and should be continued to the end of the Second World War and even beyond. Lastly, while not all Jewish pedlars were criminals, the marginality of that lifestyle and its antecedents with the roving gangs or *Betteljuden* of central and western Europe meant that there was an intricate transnational link to transgressing the law – sometimes in collective fashion. Crimes might be in the relatively minor category of dealing in stolen goods, or at the other extreme might involve violence and murder, as with the later career of Jacob Harris. In short, peddling reveals the marginal world occupied by most Jews in the early modern period and beyond, especially Jewish immigrants. Most led impoverished and vulnerable but nonetheless fascinating lives.

Researching Jewish criminality runs the risk of 'muckraking' identified by Moshe Rosman, and it would be wrong to dismiss out of hand the dilemmas associated with writing about it. In the 1980s I was part of a workshop helping to advise on what emerged as a pioneer and successful oral history of the African Caribbean community in the UK, focusing on the port of Southampton. In terms of sample, I asked if some of those on the community's margins who might have engaged in criminal activity would be included. The response was that these appeared, far more commonly than merited, in the local press. For a community under regular attack in the form of discrimination and violence, it was a perfectly understandable and totally valid reply.

It could be answered that in the media, as with the imperial law court, the 'subaltern does not speak', and that for posterity their life stories had been lost to history, or rather we get a very warped version of them. That researching criminality can be considered without too much agonising in the Jewish case reflects the passing of time since mass migration took place and, from that, a sense of security which may possibly be misplaced. I would argue it is a minor risk worth taking to understand the dynamics of the Jewish world, including those who might be regarded as nonconformists within it,[29] as well as relationships with non-Jews: such questions of past, even recent, criminality should therefore not be avoided. The picture that emerges might be messier than when presenting minorities as faultless, but it will be more human and engaging as a result. Ultimately, as 'experiments' in micro-history, these obscure and sometimes disturbing lives are fascinating and deserve to be rediscovered.

As the example from Southampton illustrates, Jews are far from alone amongst minorities, especially those of a migrant origin, in being accused of possessing innate criminality. In the Jewish case, such prejudice incorporates a religious underpinning from the ancient charge of deicide onwards. It took on a diabolical nature with the accusations of ritual murder and blood libel through which Jews in the medieval period and after have been brutally persecuted, accused of killing Jewish children as a form of human sacrifice. Indeed, there will be echoes of the blood libel and of the Jew as devil in examples within the chapters that follow. On some occasions, as with 'Jew Suss' in Germany, and a less sensational legal case in London during the 1730s which contained strong elements of the blood libel, the crimes Jews were accused of were totally imaginary and tell us only about Christian fears and anxieties.

In the nineteenth century, race science was employed to suggest that Jews were 'naturally' criminal. With the Nazi era, such tendencies to essentialise and racialise the Jews reached their climax with the Holocaust. It was, from the Jewish victim's perspective, 'the crime of my very existence'.[30] Much more common are cases where Jews were falsely and unfairly accused of dominating real crimes, where their role was much more limited than was alleged. Reflecting the insecure place of Jews, even in emerging liberal democracies, this often led to a defensive Jewish communal position and a desire either to perform self-policing, hoping to lessen any public and governmental concern, or, from the late nineteenth century onwards, to use statistics to prove that Jews were generally as law-abiding as those around them.[31] Such defensive work, by nature, was dull. It was also necessary.

The intersecting histories employed in this study will include not only other migrant groups, but also gender. There were Jewish female pedlars and Jewish female criminals, and they will certainly not be excluded from consideration here. But it remains the fact that most pedlars and most criminals were male, reflecting both wider societal trends and the specific dynamics of the Jewish world. It will thus be helpful at this stage to introduce work on Jewish masculinity and to assess how it might help inform our case studies. If work on gender has come late into Jewish studies, that on the construction of masculinity has been even more neglected.[32] Key interventions were Paul Breines's *Tough Jews* (1990) and Daniel Boyarin's *Unheroic Conduct* (1997). While covering vastly different chronologies and geographies, there is a commonality between the two: both argued that until the late modern era, when the pressure of antisemitism and the desire to conform proved irresistible, Jewish men were gentle, almost embracing effeminacy and choosing a life of learning rather than more physical, including violent, 'heroic' forms of manliness.[33]

In the case of peddling, while the occupation as a whole was male dominated, it does seem that there were proportionally far fewer Jewish women in this role than non-Jewish women. To give a snapshot in one particular year, when Elizabeth Hirsh, who it will be suggested was a close relative of Jacob Harris, applied for a pedlar's licence in 1715, there were no other Jewish women in the substantial list, even though half of those listed were female, including, remarkably, eleven women who shared her first name.[34] Far from all pedlars applied for licences, but Elizabeth Hirsh was the only Jewish woman who did so in the first decades of the eighteenth century. The pattern in that century and beyond in the UK was for the Jewish man to be the travelling pedlar and, if he was married, for his wife to be at home. This slowly broke down over time, with women becoming more involved with peddling from the late nineteenth century, often out of economic necessity through widowhood or single status.

There have been no studies of the Jewish pedlar and masculinity. Undoubtedly some men in this trade were frustrated scholars and attempted to continue their learning alongside their hard and often arduous lives on the road. It could be a dangerous life, but rather than simply being victims of violence, male Jewish pedlars were not infrequently perpetrators. Jacob Harris was in a category of his own as a triple murderer, but there were many others involved in attacks – including against each other. There are contemporary representations and writings that depict Jewish pedlars as gentle characters, and some undoubtedly were. Overall, however, they performed many types of masculinity, and did so within a wider society and specific Jewish milieu which was patriarchal and maintained gender hierarchies.

In relation to criminality, there have been assumptions both within and outside the Jewish world (including those hostile to it) that Jewish perpetrators have been non-violent, and that murder especially was extremely rare. Sarah Imhoff highlights the case in 1908 of Theodore Bingham, chief of police in New York, who falsely claimed that over half the crime in the city was committed by Jews. He also argued that Jewish men were not fit for hard labour and the crimes they committed lacked courage and aggression. Imhoff shows how the response of the leaders of New York Jewry used statistics to show the falseness of this general claim, but also how they accepted the logic of his claims about non-violent Jewish masculinity.[35]

This study will also query such assumptions and show that Jewish men, sometimes collectively, carried out violent crimes, including murder, from at least the early modern period in Europe. The model of Jewish male 'gentleness' has its limitations, even though the persistence of the claim of effeminacy will be shown to be powerful in representations of Jews and in everyday relations, running alongside fears of Jewish male sexuality. I suggest that those carrying out such violence were not manifesting 'toxic masculinity'; rather their behaviour fell within the norm of 'acceptable' forms of Jewish patriarchy.[36] Indeed, in a particular study of a one-time pedlar and smuggler turned boxer, Daniel Mendoza, I show the dangers of embracing and celebrating 'tough Jews', an attitude that can lead us to ignore often violent instances of misogyny.

Important though it is, gender will be far from the only analytical tool used to explore the lives of Jewish pedlars and criminals – class, 'race' and nation will feature as strongly. And while paying great attention to individuals, Jewish communal responses and wider histories will always be present, especially in relation to the presence of pedlars and/or criminals. I do not aim to provide an institutional history of the Jewish community of Sussex, which has its origins in the medieval period, and in the century following 1734 slowly developed a major settlement in Brighton, which at its peak in the 1960s and 1970s was over 10,000 strong. This study provides an alternative and parallel history, adding to the more traditional storytelling regarding Jewish settlement. It recognises the role of pedlars in its formation, following a pattern found elsewhere in the early years of modern British Jewry, but does so in a more critical manner, including the place of a criminal fraternity which was both a part of and apart from the wider community.

## Structure of the book

The overall approach of this book is to follow a chronological progression from the late seventeenth century onwards, weaving together the local and the transnational. In Part I, contemporary sources and the folklore that developed around the Jacob Harris murders are interrogated to establish as much as feasible about what happened and what they reveal about Harris. Not one of them can be taken at face value, hence the need to devote so much time and energy to their nature and to wider questions of knowledge exchange.

From that foundation, Part II contextualises Jacob Harris in Jewish history, including that of its institutions, and within wider Jewish/non-Jewish relations in Georgian England. The rise and geographic spread of the Jewish pedlar in the provinces – including northern England and the south-west of England into Wales – provide case studies of individuals and their relationships to burgeoning communities. From its historic foundations in the long eighteenth century, Parts III and IV follow the story to the present day, taking in the spectacular growth of Jewish migration and the tensions caused by the paper walls of immigration control that undermined it after the First World War. Part III covers the Jewish pedlar and criminal across other parts of the United Kingdom, including Ireland, and the wider British Empire in the long nineteenth century. Part IV examines the final decades of the Jewish pedlar, covering Scotland and other places where Jews, fleeing persecution and poverty in Eastern Europe and then Nazi Germany, settled in the first half of the twentieth century.

Alongside the book's ambitious chronology and geography, it never loses sight of its central character, Jacob Harris, and how wider changes in the Jewish experience and Jewish/non-Jewish relations impacted on how he was treated and represented. Context is critical in understanding the lives of Jewish pedlars and criminals. Taking the former, the means of peddling changed extensively from the eighteenth through to the twentieth century. Modes of transport – foot, cart, bike and even car – were always in flux, as were the means of selling, with credit becoming a common feature from the late nineteenth century onwards. Inevitably, the goods and services sold varied across the three centuries covered, as well as the locations. Each place had its own dynamics in which the Jews found themselves, in terms of their status and the economic development of the region. While the global ambitions of Hasia Diner's pioneer study of the Jewish pedlar are admirable, this study takes a very different perspective regarding geography and chronology. In *Roads Taken*, Diner argues that it 'tells the history of no single place or time' because she believes there was a universal Jewish pedlar experience.[37] Here heterogeneity will be to the fore, and I make no particular claim that Jewish pedlars played a key role in the transformation to industrial societies or that their activities (and those of Jewish criminals as well in a negative way) fundamentally changed Jewish/non-Jewish relations. Nevertheless, peddling and criminality are key to understanding the modern Jewish experience, and deserve attention. More modestly, my aim is to explore and recover, in a non-celebratory way, remarkable lives and experiences that are astonishing in themselves and add to our understanding of both Jewish and more general history.

Combining history *and* memory (including the legacy of the medieval era), with an ambitious chronology within a transnational approach which also embraces and insists on the importance of the local, what follows is not intended as a straightforward history. Adding further complexity, this study reflects the elaborate milieu of the Jewish pedlars and criminals and the messiness of their life stories in a fast-changing world, starting at the eve of modernity. It reflects an era when humanity was increasingly on the march within and between nation states, and then to continents beyond in the age of imperialism. The importance of migration is fundamental to this study. It will cover journeys from the continent of Europe to the United Kingdom, movement within the British Isles and then the British Empire, and finally to those remaining places in the world where Jews were still able to gain entry following the closing of doors after 1918. Through its many layers the aim is to explore, through Jacob Harris and his contemporary Jews, and others that followed their path of peddling and crime, concepts of the insider and the outsider in Europe and its empires. The starting point, however, is Ditchling Common on the evening of Sunday 28 May 1734 and the misdeeds of the UK's first and only Jewish triple murderer.

# 1

# Jacob Harris and the murders
# of 1734: the archive

1734, May the 26th. Jacob Harris, a Jew pedlar by trade, and travelling the country with his wares, having murdered at Ditchling Common, one Miles, his wife, and maid, and then plundered the house, was captured at Turner's Hill by John Oliver and his man, and committed by Mr Sergesson, before whom he was taken, to Horsham Gaol. Having been found guilty of the offence at the assizes, and condemned to die, he was hung at Horsham, August 31st, and his body afterwards removed to Ditchling Common to be hung up on a gibbet near to the house in which the murder was committed, the 2nd day of September. Many went to see him hanging; and Mr Healey preached an impressive sermon upon it the Sunday following.[1]

Here is our story in a nutshell. The authenticity of the account is confirmed, as it comes from a contemporary diary entry, written by a respectable member of the gentry from mid-Sussex who lived not far from where the terrible crime was committed. This chapter unpicks this source (in fact a partly fictitious one, as it is a reworking of an original manuscript – at this stage it is only necessary to point out that Mr Healey was no longer alive in 1734!) and others to show how hard it is to establish the 'facts' of this case. It also introduces the key players in the story and shows them to be as tricky to pin down as Harris himself. The cast of characters is fascinating and varied – including a ruthlessly ambitious politician, a corrupt judge and a print entrepreneur treading a fine line in legality. The original documentation leaves many intriguing mysteries to solve. Moreover, subsequent historians have provided false leads. Both of these challenges will have to be confronted by nimble footed detective work: a critical approach needs to be taken to almost everything that has been written, either at the time or subsequently, about the killing spree carried out by Jacob Harris. By the end of the chapter, however, it should be clear what is definitively 'knowable' about the murders and what is lost to posterity.

If our story is classic micro-history, then we should expect, as one of its key theorists, Giovanni Levi, promised, 'uncertainty, inconsistency [and] non-linearity'.[2] There is no doubt that a shocking crime *was* committed in late May 1734 on Ditchling Common. Beyond that basic 'fact', however, we will have to tread carefully in establishing even a precise chronology.[3] The primary research has by necessity been inventive and exhaustive, especially due to the loss of material over time – itself revealing of what was deemed worthy of preservation. Even so, a remarkable variety of contemporary materials *have* survived. In short, if the murders have been strangely neglected, except for a flurry of antiquarian interest in the mid-nineteenth century, this oversight is not due to a lack of sources. Indeed, for early eighteenth-century social history it is relatively abundant in contemporary documents, even if all of them, as will now emerge, are inherently slippery.

## 'Known knowns'?

The enhanced diary extract that began this chapter has been much repeated in providing an account of the murders and the capture and punishment of the perpetrator. It purports to be a transcription of John Stapley's diary. It seems ideal documentation, especially as Stapley recorded only major events in his local world. In 1733 he inherited the bulk of his father's estate, Hickstead Place, which was located less than five miles from Ditchling Common.[4] In short, we have, it seems, a straightforward, contemporary account written by a literate and well-informed man who lived in a neighbouring parish.

John Stapley was far from the first in his family to be a local chronicler. In fact, several generations of the male line of the Stapley family in the seventeenth and eighteenth centuries wrote overlapping account books and diaries. In 1866 these were edited for publication in the *Sussex Archaeological Collections*. The author of these selections was the Reverend Edward Turner, a founder member in 1846 and then senior figure in the Sussex Archaeological Society, which claims to be 'the oldest of its type in the country'.[5] When they appeared in the public realm for the first time, Turner was the private owner of the Hickstead Place archives. Here lies our first problem: Turner's 'transcriptions' could not be checked for accuracy – or indeed fabrication – by his peers.[6]

It is, in terms of historical malpractice, quite shocking that the Reverend Turner either totally invented elements of this particular diary entry or borrowed from other sources (some were relevant to this incident, others utterly unconnected to it). It could be suggested that with such inventiveness, he was a playful postmodernist before his time. To illustrate how much he reworked the original, we will now look at the *two* (rather than one) undoctored relevant entries from the Stapley diary. Stripped bare of the embellishments and fabrications of the Reverend Turner, they still provide a powerful and often unique account of the murderous crime:

> 26 May 1734: Then one Jacob Harris did murder one miles his wife and maid and the rouge was taken att turner Hill by John Oliver a mason and Mr Sergison did commit him to Horsham Gealle.

> 31 August 1734: Then Jacob Harris was hanged att Horsham for murdring 3 persons att ditchaling Common and was hung upon a Gibbet their, the second day of september.[7]

In short, the *authentic* diary entries by John Stapley neither referred to Jacob Harris as Jewish nor as a pedlar. And while it was no doubt how Turner thought things should be that another clergyman preached on the Sabbath following the murders of the terrible sins committed by the 'Jew pedlar', Mr Healey (or Healy), as noted, was in fact deceased by this time. Healy did preach nearby and was mentioned by another local diarist writing decades earlier. He thus had to be brought back from the dead and relocated so that Turner could restore Christian order to the story and rescue it from pagan misinterpretation (necessary, no doubt, in his view because of the continuing folk magic associated with the murderer's body).

As the current keeper of the Hickstead Place archives has commented, the Reverend Edward Turner's reproduction of primary evidence more generally was 'fanciful and inaccurate [and] it would not surprise me if he had embellished his account with material derived from his own preconceptions'.[8] To paraphrase Voltaire, if the itinerant 'Jew' Jacob Harris had not existed, it would have been necessary for the Reverend Turner to have invented him. Turner's version of John Stapley's diary and his commentary on it has been and continues to be *the* original text on which the telling and retelling of these murders depends. As shown, it is far from a 'reliable source' in establishing the details of the case.[9]

More generally, one of the fascinating and frustrating aspects of this remarkable story is how *all* the primary sources, when examined closely, become as unreliable as Turner's version of the Stapley diary. So are there, in the words of former United States Secretary of Defense Donald Rumsfeld,[10] any indisputably 'known knowns' in the story of Jacob Harris and his killing spree? Or is it the case that all the relevant archives and documentary materials, resting tantalisingly on the modern/premodern borderland, are inherently unstable?

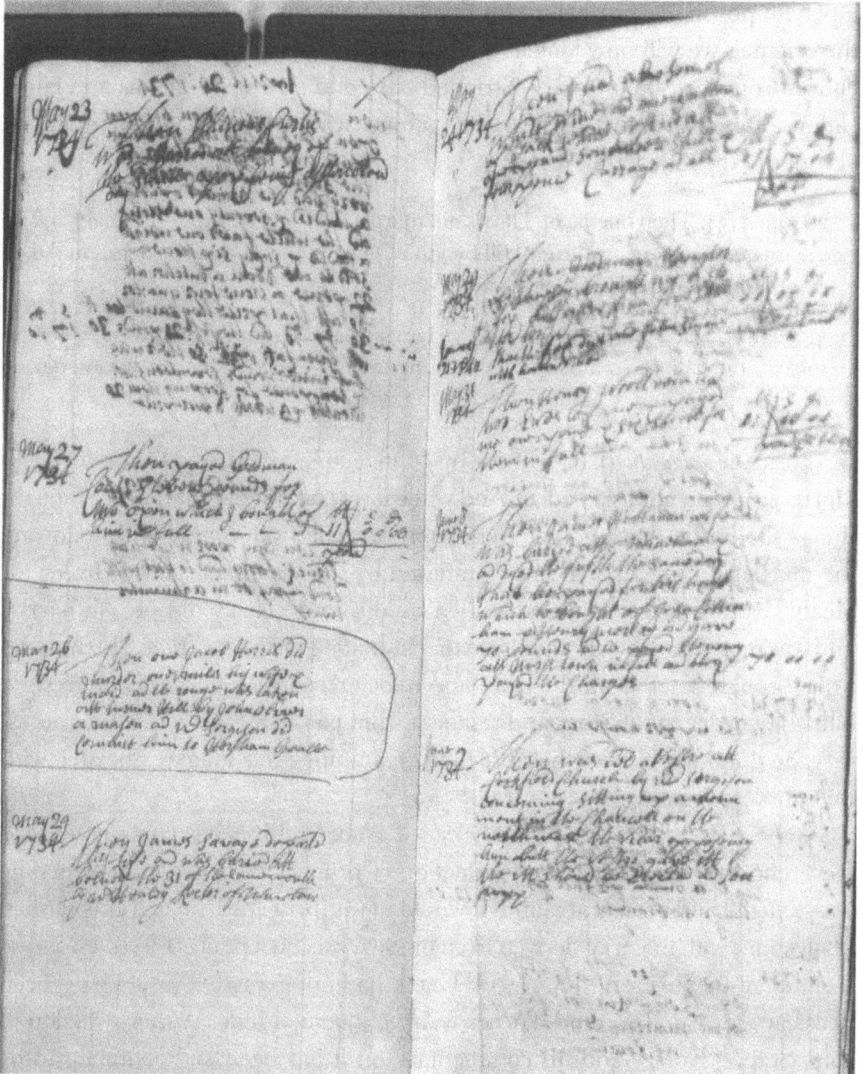

**Figure 2** Stapley diary describing the murders

There are many silences in the archive over these murders. This has led to the emergence of certain myth-making, allowing the imagination of later figures (the Reverend Turner being one of the earliest in print, but building on much earlier folk tradition) to run riot. Why Jacob Harris killed the three people in the wayside inn is one of the most enticing of these 'unknowns'. That he did it, however, despite late twentieth- and early twenty-first-century attempts to suggest otherwise, is not, in this author's view, open to serious doubt. While it seems that Harris himself pleaded his innocence, in the words of Voltaire's later and equally eloquent commentator on the human condition, model Mandy Rice-Davies, facing a certain death sentence, 'he would, wouldn't he?'[11]

Frustratingly, there are no detailed accounts of the trial itself in Horsham, or of the preceding local inquest almost certainly held in Ditchling itself, probably in the sixteenth-century coaching inn, The Bull.[12] In terms of trial publications, as J. M. Beattie notes in his definitive *Crime and the Courts in England 1660–1800* (1986), in contrast to neighbouring Surrey, only one pamphlet was printed in Sussex for the period he covers. For Surrey, pamphlet series provided graphic details of the assizes proceedings. These were sold commercially and focused on murder and rape, revealing 'intimate details of the lives of the principals involved and present[ing] opportunities for a delicious mixture of prurience and moral outrage'.[13] The only Sussex case printed concerned the notorious Hawkhurst Gang – a story of smuggling and murder which occurred a decade later. The trial details were published in 1749 and, taking eighteenth-century Sussex – indeed British – social history as a whole, the exploits of this vicious gang overshadowed the crimes of Jacob Harris.[14] They have produced much subsequent memory, the latest manifestation being Alex Preston's historical thriller, *Winchelsea*.[15] Although there are no published contemporary reports for the Ditchling Common murders, the verdict of his trial was widely reported in both the London and provincial press: this was an event worthy of *national* attention. An example of the coverage is provided by the *Country Journal* on Saturday 17 August 1734. It noted that

> On Tuesday Night last the Assizes ended at Horsham, in the County of Sussex, when the Villain who committed that barbarous Murder on Richard Miles (who kept a little Ale house near Ditchelling Common) by cutting his Throat with a Hook knife from Ear to Ear, in the stable, as he was cleaning his Horse, and afterwards murdered his Wife, who was sick in Bed, and also his Maid Servant, was capitally convicted, and received Sentence of Death; and is ordered to be hung in Chains on Ditchelling Common, facing the House where he committed the said Murder.[16]

There are subtle, but significant, variations in the way newspapers reported the outcome of the trial, especially in the way that Jacob Harris was described. In terms of detail, however, of the crimes committed they added nothing to their earlier accounts when the murders were first recorded. The variations in the reporting suggest in some cases unique 'local knowledge', to use the phrase of anthropologist Clifford Geertz,[17] but the absence of any details of the evidence produced at the trial suggests that the outcome was communicated to the press by at most one or two correspondents. As a result, and as with all other sources, the voice of Jacob Harris himself is never heard. Moreover, as the trial itself would have been incredibly brief, probably lasting a matter of minutes, it would not have provided much new detail for a burgeoning press desperate for copy to titillate and horrify its readership.

It has recently been suggested, based on the supposition of Jacob Harris's Jewishness and with a sensitivity linked to growing engagement with the Holocaust, that he became a scapegoat for the murders. As will be shown, the nature of Jewish/non-Jewish relations in Georgian England was complex, and at one extreme included antisemitic violence and even murder. At this stage it would be wrong to totally dismiss the possibility that Harris was, in fact, innocent and therefore framed because of his Jewishness. Yet when the contemporary evidence is critically examined, it still seems extremely improbable that he was anything but guilty. It is true that a large part of the evidence presented in the week following the murders emanated from one of the victims, Richard Miles. Miles was attacked on Sunday 26 May, but did not pass away until Thursday 30 May. He was conscious throughout, and in that brief period he communicated, in various forms and for different purposes, his account of what had happened. Why, however, Miles, who knew he was dying, would lie about the perpetrator of his and his wife's murders is hard to imagine. The murderer was found and brought back to be positively identified by Richard Miles – which he did without any element of doubt. It was on his evidence, and the wounds that Miles subsequently died from, that Jacob Harris was quickly found guilty.

Because of the scale and brutality of the crime, even by eighteenth-century standards where violence was an everyday part of life, the early stages of the case attracted widespread newspaper interest. As Jeremy Black notes, in the press at that time, 'interest in a good story seems to have played as large if not more of a role in the preference for inserting details of criminal activities' as 'warnings to those fearful of attack'. Whatever the purpose for its inclusion, crime was a mainstay of the press. In this respect, Black quotes a regular reader, the Earl of Essex, responding to the content of newspapers just a year after the events in Ditchling Common took place: 'I see frequent murders and robberies mentioned'.[18] While the first Sussex newspaper would not be produced until later in the century, the relative proximity of Sussex to the capital enabled the murders to reach national prominence less than a week later.

Indeed, the crime was reported as early as 31 May 1734, the day following Richard Miles's death. The first to do so was the *Penny London Post*. It gave no details of the incident other than to state that 'A dreadfull murder has been lately committed at Ditchelling near Lewes in Sussex, on Richard Miles, and Dorothy his wife, and one maid servant.' It should be noted that nowhere is the name of the servant recorded. Extensive searching in local church burial records has yielded no results: she remains the most obscure figure in this whole tragedy. Through her occupation and the fact that despite her horrendous wounds she managed to escape the crime scene suggests youthfulness. Whether or not she was local to Ditchling is unknown.[19] Rather than the victims, the focus was on a description of the murderer. He was 'a man between 20 and 30 years of age, wearing black bushy hair, a flatish nose, thick lips and about five foot seven high of middle size in bulk', who had ridden off 'upon a grey gelding about 14 hands and a half high, upon the flea-bit'.[20]

The reasons for such detail, which extended into the exact attire worn by the murderer, was that he was still assumed to be at large and needed to be caught, both for the public good and for the sake of justice. Indeed, the cost of this publicity was listed by the county of Sussex in the expenses later to be repaid by the Treasury. Information for the London press often came by post, and there were only three deliveries a week.[21] This explains why it took until the first day of June 1734 for the newspapers to give much more up-to-date and detailed information on the murders.

One of the fullest of these accounts – not just of the murders, but of their immediate aftermath – was produced in the *London Evening Post*.[22] It is thus worth quoting at length, especially as other newspapers copied it and it almost certainly provided the details on which the long-lasting ballad of the crime was based. And although the grotesque details were no doubt intended to entertain the readers – there is thus a danger even now in reproducing the report's gothic horror and insensitivity – it is still important in trying to establish not only what happened but also the sheer bloodiness and brutality of the crimes committed. Ultimately, while all attempts will be made in this study to restore agency to Jacob Harris, this objective cannot and should not disguise the nature of what he did that late spring evening in 1734. There remains a risk that the passing of close to three centuries might camouflage his actions in some romantic haze, especially when the intriguing question of just who Jacob Harris was is raised. Folk hero or not, even if from a marginalised minority, the utter horror of his actions is indisputable. The flurry of the attacks and their chaotic nature has the feel of a badly acted West End farce moving from one scene of disaster to another. The reality, however, was anything but comic.

The *London Evening Post* was founded in 1727. It was one of the most vigorous of a new breed of 'tri-weekly papers, called Evening Posts and produced [in the capital] on the post days'.[23] Its reporting of the murders was certainly relentless in its energy. It would have been based on local intelligence relying on Miles's testimony, which in turn was communicated by letter to London:

> On Sunday last between Nine and Ten o'Clock in the evening a barbarous Murder was committed, at a little Ale-house by a Common, in the Parish of Ditchelling near Lewes in the County of Sussex, by a Fellow well-dress'd, and with a good Horse, who had lodged two Nights at the said Ale-house: He went out with the Man of the House, whose Name was Richard Miles, into the Stable; and while he was doing something to the Fellow's Horse, he came slyly behind him, and with a Pocket-Knife cut his Throat almost through the Windpipe; then, thinking he had done his Business, he went into the Man's House, and meets the Maid at the Bottom of the Chamber Stairs, and cut her Throat in two Places from Ear to Ear, and gave her a deep Stab in the Breast, notwithstanding she got out of the House, and ran down a Field; but getting over a Stile, was suppos'd to fall into a Ditch, where she was found dead of her Wounds: Then he went up Stairs to the Man's Wife, who was sick a Bed, and cut her Throat from Ear to Ear, into the very Bone through her Windpipe, who was also found dead on the Floor in the Chamber lying in her Gore.

In a line that, significantly, was to be replicated in *The Ballad of Jacob Harris*, the *London Evening Post* concluded that the dead wife was 'a most dismal Object to behold'.[24] The maid, it was reported somewhat pruriently (hints of a sexual element to the violence can be found in other reporting), 'hearing her Master cry out in the Stable, wrapp'd her Gown loose round her', and was found 'only in her Shirt, and the said Gown round her'.[25]

The account did not end here. Indeed, the level of excitement was then intensified: 'the Man who was first wounded, notwithstanding his Loss of Blood, got to a Neighbour's House, and rais'd the Family, who came in so hastily upon the Murderer, that he took his Horse and made off, without taking any Thing but the Man's Pocket Money, which was about 40 or 50s'.[26] At the point when the account was first penned, the reader was left hanging: 'The Man's Wounds were sew'd up, but his Life is very much doubted of.'[27] In fact, on 29 May 1734, three days after the attack, Richard Miles was just about strong enough to rewrite his will, commenting that while he was of 'perfe[c]t mind and memory' he was 'seriously worried to the Endanger of my Life an in a very weak (and low of life) in body'.[28] Adding to the fluidity of all the principal characters, this legal document revealed that the victim's name was also mutable, and had been Richard Page in an earlier manifestation.[29]

The *London Evening Post* included further details of the murderer provided by Richard Miles: 'he is a Smuggler, and has been at his House several Times before; but he knows not any other Name he has but James'.[30] With the arrival of fresh correspondence, an afterword to the article provided readers with the sad, but also reassuring outcome to the crime: 'We hear the Rogue is since taken, and being brought before the poor Man (who is since dead) he declared him to be the Murderer; upon which he is committed to Horsham Gaol, in order to be try'd at the next Assizes.'[31]

From this narrative, it is evident that Miles had an ongoing relationship with the murderer and that the crime was certainly not one committed by an unknown and opportunist intruder. That connection complicates the story and reveals much about the lives of both victim and perpetrator. Even so, it does not cast doubt on who had carried out the triple murder. This was from the start an exceptional moment, as was reflected in the burial registers of Wivelsfield Church, the nearest Christian place of worship to the scene of the crime and the focal point of a tiny hamlet of that name. The third entry for 1734 reads 'Richard Miles an Dorithy his wife *murdered an* Was Buried hear June 1'.[32] The two words in italics were in the same hand but appear to have been added in the register a little later, despite there being little space to do so.[33] Recording baptisms, marriages and burials was a legal requirement of parish churches, and had been since the Reformation for political and religious reasons.[34] Noting that individuals had been murdered was not. The burial register in Wivelsfield Church thereby emphasises the extraordinary nature of the crime, but again adds another level of chronological disorderliness in our contemporary primary sources as the original entry was embellished.

While there is no pamphlet or substantial newspaper coverage of Jacob Harris's trial, the historian *is* extremely lucky that the coroner's reports which outline the crimes survive in full.[35] That their occurrence took place on the cusp of modernity has already been noted – at a point when the approaches to crime and punishment in England were slowly changing.[36] One indirect result was that these murders were recorded not only by what was now a fast-expanding and frequent newspaper industry, but also within the state bureaucratic archive at a county level and later within national record keeping. Indeed, it has been highlighted how 'The earliest case of capital punishment at Horsham of which private and published, in addition to official, particulars are found is that of Jacob Harris, the pedlar.'[37]

In Ditchling on 30 May 1734, 'upon view of the body of Richard Miles then and there lying', thirteen jurors of Ditchling and 'four other Villages next adjoining' swore 'when where how and in what manner [the victim] came by his Death'.[38] Aside from the then private Hickstead Place archive, this was the first document that referred to the perpetrator and his deeds using the name by which he would subsequently largely be identified. Even then, the coroner's reports did so indirectly and incompletely: 'Jacob' and 'Harris' do not appear contiguously as they do in John Stapley's diary entry. The indictment was that

> James otherwise Jacob Hirsh otherwise Harris late of the parish ... not having the fear of God before his eyes but being moved and seduced by the Instigation of the Devil on the six and twentieth day of May ... feloniously wilfully and of his malice ... did make an assault and ... the said James otherwise Jacob Hirsh otherwise Harris with a certain knife of the value of two [pence] made of Iron & steel ... held in his right hand ... did strike & cut ... Richard Miles ... Throat [with] two mortal wounds of the length of each of them of three inches and of the depth of two Inches ... Richard Miles ... did languish and languishing did live on [until the] thirtieth day of May.[39]

This legal document adds further to our understanding that the naming (and from this the identity) of the murderer was varied, uncertain and complex. From this evidence, James/Jacob Hirsh/Harris was delivered to Horsham gaol to await the next assizes, which took place on 12 August, a wait of over two months.[40] Presided over by John Michell, who was county coroner for East Sussex from 1710 to 1734,[41] four of the original jurors, with a further three (including John Oliver who, according to the diarist John Stapley, had captured the murderer in Turner's Hill), provided largely the same information. They added, however, that Hirsh/Harris 'feloniously did break and enter' Miles's house, putting his wife Dorothy in 'corporal fear of her life' and also stealing 'one Ryding Coat of the value of Ten shillings'.[42]

Hirsh/Harris was found guilty of the murder but 'not Guilty [of] breaking the house'. Given the severity of the former crime, the latter was irrelevant in terms of the certain capital punishment Jacob Harris would receive. That he was officially found not guilty of theft does not necessarily have any larger significance – either in terms of the murderer's motives or his innocence in this respect. To pursue the possibility of theft would have only prolonged and complicated the trial. Likewise, the fact that Hirsh/Harris was described in these legal documents as 'late of the parish [of Ditchling] and ... [a] Labourer' is of little import.[43] As Beattie clarifies, the clerks drawing up such documents 'wanted to ensure that the indictment would not be rejected by the court as being improperly drawn up'. Instead, they 'opted for the forms that had been found acceptable over decades of trial and error'. They described 'virtually every defendant as a "labourer", using a broad status designation rather than a precise occupation; and they invariably listed his place of residence as the parish in which the crime had taken place'.[44] In this respect, the official archive relating to Jacob Harris fits the norm perfectly. It leaves open his occupation(s), and whether he had a sense of belonging to Ditchling or not.

According to the coroner's records, on Tuesday 13 August 1734 (although many newspapers stated that it was three days earlier) Hirsh/Harris was found guilty. The Gaol Delivery Calendar for Horsham recorded that he and another criminal, Edward Saires (who was accused of breaking and entry and the theft of goods to the value of five shillings), 'must be severely hanged by their necks untill they be dead'.[45] Saires, however, as was the case for many such drastic punishments for minor crimes in the eighteenth century, was reprieved. Unfortunately for Jacob Harris, a triple murderer was never going to be dealt with so 'leniently'.[46]

After several months during which Hirsh/Harris had been languishing in gaol, with the trial and then the verdict newspaper interest in the case revived. While the reports they provided add further to the coroner's reports, they can be queried in terms of both detail and chronology. In the original version of John Stapley's diary and in all later narratives, it is assumed that Harris was hanged in Horsham on 31 August 1734 and then his body was transported to Ditchling Common and the scene of the crime to be gibbeted there. In the newspaper accounts, all of which were produced in the last week of August, it was reported that the murderer,

> James Jacob Daves, alias Harris who was condemned at the last Assizes at Horsham … was executed on a Gibbet at Ditchelling Common in Sussex, for the Murder of Richard Miles, his Wife and Servant Maid. He was afterwards hanged in Chains on the said Gibbet, pursuant to his Sentence.[47]

This account from the *Daily Journal* dated the gibbeting to 24 August 1734. Clearly Stapley, as a neighbouring contemporary, believed that the murderer had been hanged first before his body was transported to Ditchling Common and this has become the accepted narrative thereafter. Local knowledge as represented by Stapley's diary and *The Ballad of Jacob Harris*, which described the murders and was circulated at the time, is almost certainly right, but some further credence is given to the press reports of where his hanging took place by the ambiguous narrative contained in the Sheriff's Cravings for the mid-1730s. This was the financial demand met by the Treasury for the costs of such major criminal cases and then paid back to the relevant county, in this case claimed by the coroner, John Michell, in Sussex. The Sheriff's Cravings relating to 1734 expenses provides precise costings for the murders in Ditchling Common. These costings add further detail to our 'known knowns' while questioning others that might be placed in that category.[48]

They covered expenses which were not specific to Jacob's trial such as the judges' lodgings at the two Sussex assizes in 1734 which totalled £30, a large sum (over £3,500 in today's currency) that suggests they were given the best accommodation and food. The expenditure relating to Jacob Harris came under six headings, the first of which was the housing and feeding of the murderer in Horsham gaol, a bill which came to £1 10s. The parsimoniousness of this amount, both in absolute and relative terms, reflects the barbarity of Jacob's prison experiences. Horsham prison was the first for the county, established in the 1540s. It was rebuilt and repaired in a haphazard way in the seventeenth century, deteriorating further as its use intensified in the next. In 1774 John Howard, the prison reformer, regarded it as a particularly appalling example in his damning report to Parliament: 'The wards are dark, dirty, and small and in no way proportioned to the number of unhappy persons confined there. There is not the least outlet for felons or debtors but the poor unhappy creatures are ever confined without the least breath of fresh air.' A year later it was agreed to rebuild Horsham gaol, but this was three decades after Jacob Harris had languished there.[49] He was also unfortunate in that the mass escape of prisoners from the gaol occurred five years after he had been hanged at the end of his incarceration in this notorious prison.[50] He must have known that capital punishment was inevitable. Whether he contemplated breaking out of Horsham gaol is unknown.

The second expenditure was the costs of guards and attendants in the 'Excurson of Hirshal Harris for the murder of 3 prisoners', which totalled £6 6s. Presumably this was to take him back to Ditchling to be identified and then to Horsham to await his trial – but the record is unclear on the geographic specifics. Indeed, the items were not listed in the chronological order in which the costs were incurred, adding an element of confusion. They are designed to be precise about the costs incurred and to aid repayment, not to provide a clear timeline. They were also requested a year after the crime itself. What is revealing, however, is its naming of the perpetrator. It is the only official document to give his surname *only* as Harris and likewise unique in giving 'Hirshal' as his first name.[51]

The third costing is more precise, which was the cost of a 'car' and attendants 'for carrying him to Ditchling being abt 20 miles & for hanging him on a Gibbet'. The cost for this was smaller than for the earlier transport at only £4 10s. The next item was an invoice for the hanging. The whole of this craving was abbreviated and the person paid £5 5s for carrying it out is described in the document as simply 'Jaes Cw', suggesting that John Michell was familiar with the man who had this unfortunate but lucrative occupation. The fifth costing casts a little doubt over whether the murderer was hanged in Horsham or at the scene of the crime – the costs were not only for 'Erecting the Gibbet' but also for the 'Galws [gallows] abt it', which totalled £6 10s. It is possible that the murderer's dead body was rehung on adjacent gallows before being placed in a gibbet, but it is also feasible that he was hanged near the inn where he had committed the triple murders.[52] It is more likely that Jacob was hanged in Horsham – he would have been a form of public entertainment, first alive, and then dead. Hangings could be attended by 'hundreds, sometimes thousands of people' in what was 'locally nick-named "The Horsham Hang Fair"'.[53]

The final item in fact related to the first costs incurred in the cycle of this law enforcement: 'For distributing Press warr[an]ts to the Constables & Hand burroughs thro' the County', initially paid for by Richard Miles. This cost £5 5s, and this large amount might help explain both the publicity that the case soon achieved, and perhaps the speed with which the murderer was caught some distance from the crime scene – especially as it was in a county notorious for its limited and atrocious roads.[54] All in all, this was an expensive case. Remarkably, it was one fifth of the total amount claimed back by the county from the Treasury for 1734 – an indication again of the exceptional nature of the crime and its punishment.[55]

To sum up so far: while the contemporary, datable documentation is relatively plentiful and revealing, there remain many uncertainties and unanswered questions, especially concerning the motives of the crime and the background of the murderer and his victims. This precariousness extends also to the details of the trial and the exact chronology and geography of what happened afterwards, including the gibbeting. It turns out, returning to Donald Rumsfeld's attempt at epistemology, that the 'known knowns', which he defines as the 'things we know we know', prove to be relatively few and far between. At this point it will be helpful to interrogate again the Stapley diary to see if any more can be gleaned from it in ascertaining exactly what happened. It is through the chance survival of the Stapley archive that we learn details of Jacob Harris and his punishment.

## The Stapley diary, the Sergisons and local patriotism

The Stapley diary confirms the exceptional nature of this crime and its prominent place in local society and culture. It adds to our understanding of how and where Harris was caught, and that his gibbeting in Ditchling Common was a moment of significance in the wider neighbourhood. The chronology it provides, however, cannot be treated as totally definitive, and its source material may have been from the national press as well as (most definitely) local knowledge in inspiration. The diary confirms, as do all the apparently exactly datable contemporary sources relating to Jacob Harris and his triple murders, the insight of another Jewish outsider when confronting the nature of the modern world over a century later. As Marx wrote in the *Communist Manifesto*: 'All that is solid melts into air.'[56]

Keeping to the family tradition, John Stapley's diary was hardly a confessional document – 'facts' are produced without comment. The entries were terse and relatively infrequent – there were just fifteen for the whole of 1734, which was one of his most productive years with the pen.[57] Almost all of these entries related to local events and formed a calendar of births, marriages, deaths and reports of ill health (including that of 'my poor wife [who] was struck from head to foot with dead palsee', a detail recorded a month before the murders). The adjective describing his spouse is the closest to an emotional response in the whole of Stapley's diary.[58] Unlike the Reverend Edward Turner's version, John Stapley, like so many of his age, did 'not overtly assign meaning, nor come to conclusions'.[59] More generally, as Felicity Nussbaum suggests, the diary 'is the thing itself, not a failed version of autobiography … The diary delivers narrative and frustrates it; it simultaneously displays and withholds.' This is the case with the entries relating to the Ditchling Common murders.[60]

The only exception to these largely familial diary entries was one shortly after that recording the triple murder. It concerned a controversy at Cuckfield Church (a neighbouring village to Ditchling some four miles away) where Mr Sergison had wanted a monument to be erected. The vicar, the Reverend Daniel Walter, opposed it as he believed that its prominence would overshadow the altar. John Stapley noted that in the end the church authorities had sided with Sergison and that the memorial 'should be Erected and sett upp'.[61] The Sergisons were long established in the area. They were wealthy landowners and became a family of great local power and influence, as was shown in the final decision over the monument – Walter was no minor figure and the historian of the village has outlined how he 'dominated Cuckfield for nearly half a century' (1713–61).[62]

Walter's objections were not without foundation – the memorial is architecturally out of place and dominates the thirteenth-century Gothic church interior, overshadowing the altar.[63] Thomas Sergison, as Stapley's diary entry for 26 May 1734 makes clear, had played a key role in committing Jacob Harris to Horsham gaol and was most likely integral to sending out information leading to his capture at Turner's Hill a few days after the crime. Indeed, his efficiency in finding and dealing with the murderer reflected a wider ambition to get himself noticed, in this case almost certainly as the local Justice of the Peace. And yet, as with the perpetrator and his first victim, the Mr Sergison referred to by John Stapley was a man who also possessed different names, a reflection again of his desire to make his mark not just in Sussex but in wider society and politics.

There was a very good reason why Sergison had persisted in his desire to erect a monument in Cuckfield Holy Trinity Church. It was in memory of Sir Charles Sergison, a former Member of Parliament and prominent figure in the organisation of the Royal Navy, who had died in 1732. Sergison had no direct heirs and had bequeathed his substantial estate around Cuckfield and well beyond across the county of Sussex to Thomas Warden, his great-nephew. There was only one condition, however – that Warden change his surname to Sergison, which he did by act of parliament. Warden/Sergison used his wealth and influence to overcome the objections of the vicar, and a monument was erected to honour Charles Sergison's many virtues – his 'intelligence, integrity, fidelity, diligence, patriotism, neighbourliness … and kindness'.[64] Thomas took up many of the responsibilities of Charles Sergison, building up the substantial estate through ruthless buying up of land.[65] He was also determined to follow the path of his great-uncle in the realm of politics. In this he was successful: Thomas became MP for Lewes in 1747 and remained so until his death in 1766.[66]

Sergison was indeed a political player, determined to win the seat of Lewes, the county town of Sussex, some thirteen miles from his main estate in Cuckfield. Campaigning for the 1734 election started a year earlier and was closed in Sussex on 10 May, just weeks before the triple murders in Ditchling Common which Sergison helped prosecute. He faced the candidates of the Duke of Newcastle, later to be Whig Prime Minister.[67] Newcastle's nominees narrowly won in 1734, those entitled to vote numbering in the low hundreds.[68] Sergison tried again in 1741, appealing in various leaflets to the 'Freeholders of the County of Sussex', but still lost by a small margin.[69]

Finally, in 1747 Newcastle did not have the funds to contest so extensively against his persistent and pesky opponent. Sergison came to an agreement with the Duke and was elected unopposed, though he had to agree to be the aristo-crat's candidate. Sergison simply wanted a seat in the Commons and what that represented in prestige and access to power, rather than having any desire to pursue wider political objects.[70] The electoral victory in 1747 thus reflected the remarkable rise, wealth, standing, determination and sheer talent of Thomas Sergison, who had previously been a lawyer in the Middle Temple in London.[71] Sergison thus had more important matters in mind at the time of the Ditchling Common murders, but he was also willing to use the power newly available to him locally to make his mark, as he did in insisting on erecting the Sergison monument. While few of his descendants matched his drive and grim determi-nation to gain wealth, power and influence, he further established the family as major force in Sussex and beyond. Jacob Harris was thus unfortunate in being a fugitive from the law at the exact point that the person representing local authority was a man determined to go places.

Sergison's emphasis on local patriotism in relation to his opponent, the Duke of Newcastle, raises the question of where Jacob Harris and his victim Richard Miles would have fitted within Sussex society. Miles was able to draw upon neighbours to seek medical help and sound the alarm. It was mainly Ditchling people who gave evidence and acted as jurors in the prosecution of Jacob Harris. One exception was probably Sergison's 'man', John Oliver, who we noted was employed to find and catch Jacob Harris some distance away from the scene of the crime. Described as a 'mason' in the Stapley diary, he is also listed in the assizes record as giving evidence of Jacob Harris's crimes in his trial, along with four witnesses.[72]

It is possible that this is the same John Oliver born in Chiddingly in East Sussex who died in Hurstpierpoint in 1759, four miles from Ditchling and a sim-ilar distance from Sergison's estate in Cuckfield.[73] Intriguingly, this John Oliver was related to Sergison through marriage.[74] This would be very neat, but it is clear from his will that *this* John Oliver was a miller. Perhaps as likely was John Oliver (1693–1741) of Ardingly (close to Turner's Hill), who may have had law-enforcing powers in the locality.[75] If so, it suggests the strong local knowledge of the diarist as a large landowner who was well connected. A third contender was John Oliver of Highdown Hill near Worthing, remembered locally by some 'as crazy, others as remarkably pious, others as a joker, others as a rogue'. The last category, appropriately for this study, came from his reputation of being a leading smuggler, living as he did so close to the Sussex coast. He died in 1793 but had built his lavish tomb in 1766 which was 'covered with passages from scripture and hieroglyphical figures'.[76]

In contrast to some of the key players in our murder narrative, it seems unlikely that the John Oliver referenced in the Stapley diary was known under a different name. *Which* John Oliver it was, however, remains uncertain. To sum up so far with regard to John Stapley's diary, it is a 'reliable' source, providing unique information on the murders, but equally frustrating in its lack of detail.

On the surface, the involvement of local witnesses might suggest that Richard Miles enjoyed a strong degree of local integration and many contacts, which his status as innkeeper would have confirmed. This does not mean, however, that Miles was simply an honest, totally law-abiding citizen.[77] On the other hand, there was certainly no place for a 'rogue' such as Jacob when it came to murder, but those involved with smuggling (which, as we have noted, Harris was accused of by Miles in drawing up the press warrants to help find his attacker) were often viewed very positively. They provided the benefits of cheaper goods through what was subversively called 'free trade' against government attempts at taxation.[78] That smuggling was an activity far from beyond the pale of respectability was shown in the 1734 Lewes election when a self-confessed smuggler offered his vote to candidates who would be lenient towards his 'trade'. Others, equally remarkably, wrote to Newcastle asking for the release of smuggler friends from the same gaol that Harris would enter a few weeks after the 1734 poll had closed.[79]

It remains that consolidating his estate and gaining a seat in Parliament were Thomas Sergison's main objectives. His local legal obligations, including that of dealing with Jacob Harris, would have been important for his prestige and local standing, and followed on neatly from his employment in the Middle Temple.[80] Significantly, his surviving papers focus only on the paperwork needed to claim his new name and status in 1732 and subsequent land purchases. There is nothing that survives relating to the Sussex assizes, including the jailing of Jacob Harris. It is thus only through the Stapley diaries that this connection to our murderer is revealed. Stapley, who lived a few miles away from Sergison in Cuckfield and was a fellow landholder who had also recently inherited his estate, was aware of the heated controversy concerning the memorial in the Holy Trinity Church, as well as the more sensational triple murder.

On the surface, John Stapley appears to be a chronicler whose first-hand sources came *only* from the locality. His world appears a smaller one than that of Thomas Sergison. Yet however simple Stapley's diary entries appear, there are deeper complexities to them that reflect the multilayered nature of this genre. While it is true that the diary was 'largely a private document in the seventeenth and early eighteenth century' (and those of the Hickstead estate were clearly not designed with an audience beyond the family in mind, highlighting major moments in his relatives' life cycle, financial accounts and 'big' local moments), these are still difficult documents to decode. All we know about John Stapley and his view of Jacob Harris's misdeeds is that he felt them to be of sufficient importance to record them not once, but twice, neatly bookended with the date of the murders at one end and the hanging and gibbeting of the perpetrator at the other. Later, these diaries and the wider Stapley archive were seen as rare and significant enough for the antiquarian Turner to preserve them and write about their contents. The genealogical longevity and relatively substantial landholding of the Stapley family meant that they met the normal remit of the Sussex Archaeological Society. There are, however, two further reflections on Stapley's diary writing practice which must be considered.

The first is that of chronology. In both cases, Stapley clearly wrote the entries some time after the date they refer to. The first, 26 May 1734, was indeed the day of the murders, but the information it contains compresses details that covered the better part of a week. Conversely, the entry under 31 August 1734 covers details of the hanging of Jacob Harris that day, but also his gibbeting two days later. It seems very likely that John Stapley wrote all his diary entries relatively close to the events he described, but not on the day he places them under (and certainly not for the two relating to Jacob Harris as they provide information that was not yet known on those dates).

The second consideration relates to an entry of 25 October 1734: 'There was an Earthquake in England[,] many people did feel itt and it was about three a clock in the morning.'[81] Such an unusual event merited a mention in Stapley's diary as much as the murders in Ditchling Common. That the earthquake is recorded as a national event shows his general knowledge of its severity, which must have come from reading newspapers (or from conversing with people who had done so).[82] It is thus just possible that his narrative of the murders was also informed by the press, but it is also the case that he provided details (for example, the role of John Oliver and Mr Sergison, and that Harris was caught at Turner's Hill) which were not recorded in any other contemporary document.[83] Likewise, the dates given for the gibbeting in Ditchling Common do not appear elsewhere at the time, and reflect that this would have been a major event – indeed a traumatic moment – in the local world. One final element remains from the Stapley diary – the description of Jacob Harris as a 'rouge' [sic].[84] The juxtaposition of the third and fourth letters suggests perhaps his own labelling of the criminal, although equally it was a word used extensively in the initial press reports and often misspelt. The term is, however, the only indication of

John Stapley's disdain for Jacob Harris and his categorising of the murderer as a criminal outsider.

The next stage is to confront the primary evidence without date or contemporary archive form.

## Known unknowns or unknown unknowns?

To Donald Rumsfeld, 'known unknowns' are things 'we know we do not know'.[85] This section considers a source that is of critical significance to the narrative and its later preservation – the 'Ballad of Jacob Harris' (also known as the 'Ballad of Jacob Hirsch'). There are many folk legends associated with the murders and their locations are numerous. They are, however, undatable and will be dealt with later. A much stronger case can be made for the first appearance of the Ballad, even if a small element of uncertainty remains as to when it was first penned and then circulated. Some of it may have been created (or elaborated) by later observers, but there is compelling evidence that it was not simply a Victorian invention.[86]

The 'Ballad of Jacob Harris' consists of sixty-three lines, and to perform it fully takes close to eight minutes – a substantial musical endeavour.[87] Such ballads played an important role in transmitting culture orally from the late medieval period onwards, but by the late twentieth century they were a genre beyond their time. As Gordon Hall, a Sussex folk singer, noted in 1996: 'No one wants to listen to them, they bore you to bloody tears unless you're interested.'[88]

It is more than likely that the verses of the Ballad were hastily assembled, probably in London, and printed as a single sheet. They would then have been sold at the site of the gibbeting for a penny, as was normally the case with such broadsides. They would be purchased by the crowds assembling for an event that was a popular attraction, resembling more a fair with a carnival atmosphere where food and drink were sold, rather than a sombre gathering. In larger towns and cities, up to 40,000 might attend a gibbeting.[89] That at Ditchling Common would have been a smaller affair, but would have attracted, by word of mouth, many from surrounding villages. It was, for example, 'doubtless attended by Cuckfield people'.[90] While thousands of these ballad broadsides were, given their ephemeral nature, 'miraculously preserved and lovingly studied' and are now part of international, digitised collections, an even greater number have been lost to posterity. Sadly, in our case no original broadsides survive, a reflection of the remoteness of Ditchling Common.[91] In 1923, local journalist, historian and conservationist Arthur Beckett fictionalised the story of the triple murders, adding at the end that he 'had in his possession a copy of the old country ballad' relating to 'Jacob the Jew'.[92] Beckett sustained a long interest in the events of 1734, printing a full version of the Ballad at the time of its bicentenary, including the description of Harris as a 'Jew rogue'. Beckett surely would have referenced the original broadside had it been available. It is frustrating that although Sussex was a major point of focus for the folk song collectors of the nineteenth and early twentieth centuries, this ballad does not appear in any of their published anthologies for the county. As noted, the largely London-based collectors tended only to go to accessible places, and Ditchling was somewhat off the route – Ditchling Common even more so.[93]

The first surviving, but partial, printed form of the 'Ballad of Jacob Harris' was published in 1856 through the popular journal, *Notes and Queries*. It was part of a short contribution from the prominent antiquarian, friend of the Reverend Edward Turner and fellow founder member of the Sussex Archaeological Society, R. W. Blencowe.[94] The particular discussion, which was long-lasting and reported across the British Isles, concerned the location of 'the last Gibbet in England'. Rather than, as claimed, being in the north-east of England and recently destroyed, Blencowe stated that it was in fact to be found on Ditchling Common relating to the hanging in chains of 'The Jew, Jacob'.[95]

Blencowe condensed the Ballad to fourteen lines. It consisted, in his words, of 'some very rude verses [which were] still preserved in the neighbourhood'.[96] Blencowe lived in Lewes, some ten miles away from the scene of what he called 'this frightful massacre'.[97] It seems likely that he wrote down or copied the Ballad having visited the district where the crime was committed, though there is nothing surviving in his archive to prove this. As his papers include ephemera, including riddles and verses he had collected, the absence of a printed or transcribed copy of the 'Ballad of Jacob Harris' is simply bad fortune for the later historian. Blencowe had wide interests including popular folklore, and was less preoccupied with producing genealogies of the local gentry and their properties than many of his contemporaries.[98] His fellow members of the Sussex Archaeological Society in the next decade reproduced only some of the verses transcribed by Blencowe in *Notes and Queries*, but tantalisingly they did not add to them.[99] The Ballad was not published in full until 1934, the bicentenary of the murders, by the local newspaper, the *Mid-Sussex Times*.[100] A rival and slightly (but significantly) different version was published five years later in the *Sussex County Magazine*.[101]

It is possible that the survival of the 'Ballad of Jacob Harris' depended to some extent on oral tradition, being passed from generation to generation by recitation. It is perhaps more likely that the printed broadside survived in some households, or that it was written down more informally. It is an interesting case study in the debate about oral or written transmission. Certainly, the persistence of the Ballad reveals the importance of the story in the locality. No doubt it would be subject to change and vary over the centuries from family to family or copy to copy. And some of the verses were common to other, earlier ballads, including its opening lines:

Good people all I pray now lend an ear,
Unto these lines which I shall now declare.

This standardisation strengthens the case that it was constructed opportunistically by those that made a living by printing and selling such broadsides in the neighbourhood where such a sensational event had occurred. If the Ballad is then taken as a contemporary document, and the contents of the two published versions from the 1930s are put alongside one another in content, is any fresh light shed on this episode that is not 'known' in other contemporary sources?[102]

As noted, the contemporary press provided much of the detail for the Ballad. Given that few copies of eighteenth-century newspapers would survive, this would seem to further support the idea that the Ballad was indeed written in the summer of 1734 after Jacob Harris had been convicted of the murders. Having established the date of the crime, the Ballad moved on to its exact timing and location:

A dreadful murder done at eventide
In Ditchling just by the common side.

The Ballad then provided a new perspective not provided by the press – that the first victim, Richard Miles, was 'a man … known full well'. That Miles was able to call for help quickly in a remote area and put into motion the apprehending and prosecution of Jacob Harris suggests that this was indeed the case. Miles could also call upon local people to execute his will, and likewise as we have noted there were many from Ditchling and neighbouring villages able to act as witnesses for the coroner's report.[103] What is less certain is the content of a later verse about Richard Miles's alehouse:

Being near the road many people there did go
To drink or lodge in this house indeed.

It is not clear when the inn became known as the Royal Oak – probably by the end of the eighteenth century, and it kept this name until its demolition in 2017. The inn was in an isolated position within Ditchling Common, which itself was remote from the village from which it took its name. There was some passing trade generated by what were, until later in the eighteenth century, often unusable roads, but the pub struggled for its existence throughout its at least 300-year history. And the very fact that Jacob Harris carried out the murders when the inn was, in early evening, deserted, casts some doubt on its popularity in 1734.

As with the Stapley diary, the Ballad names the murderer as 'Jacob by name', but in this case the source does not provide a surname. The two published versions from the 1930s differ in how the murderer's identity is constructed, though both insist on describing him three times as 'this rogue', suggesting he was not perceived as truly belonging to the locality. In terms of the familiarity of the murderer with his first victim, the Ballad went further and suggested that Jacob 'oftentimes for lodging thither came', which to some extent questions his otherness to Ditchling Common. Whether this idea of Harris's familiarity with the inn came from local knowledge or simply extrapolation from the newspaper reports is now hard to judge, but the fact that this connection was preserved in folk tradition suggests further an ongoing relationship between Harris and Miles.

The heart of the Ballad was devoted to the three murders themselves, sparing the listener none of the gore. It starts with the killing of Richard Miles – the

> ruffian … cut his throat across from ear to ear
> And threw his body up against the wall.

The sheer *physical strength* of Jacob Harris is notable, and this has been confirmed as an outstanding feature by a police detective sergeant re-examining the evidence of these crimes more recently.[104] No motive for Harris, however, is given in the Ballad other than his desire 'to murder all', having (he thought) disposed of the innkeeper. It is only the violence and uncontrolled anger of Jacob Harris (the 'murdering rogue') that is emphasised in the Ballad. He takes Richard Miles's horse, but only to escape from the crime scene. In fact, that Harris is not accused of stealing the horse in the charges drawn against him by the coroner suggests that this was Jacob's own animal, a significant detail. What happened to the horse is never referred to: the coroner's inquest stated that 'he had no chattels'.[105]

The Ballad continues with the maid, who had been alerted to the crime by her master's cry. Running down the stairs to investigate, Jacob

> met her there his spleen to show't
> He stabbed her twice and cut her throat.

40

It is intriguing that details provided by the press – that Jacob had stabbed the maid in the breast and that she was in a state of undress when she escaped – were not reproduced in the Ballad. That Jacob Harris had murdered two women in cold blood is not, of course, ignored, but the Ballad does not hint at a *sexualised* discourse to describe the nature of the crimes committed. In this respect, there is a contrast to the more salacious newspaper reports.

The servant's 'dame' is allocated only one line: 'He threw her … and cut her throat also'.[106] It is probable that by this stage the author of the Ballad was running out of space, and with much more to relate, Dorothy and her servant's deaths were given little attention. Equally, gender and class considerations may also have played a role in their neglect. Having confirmed that 'The women both that night this world forsook', the attention now focused on 'poor Miles' and Jacob himself. Again, whether through guesswork or local information, the Ballad provides details of Harris's capture that are not confirmed elsewhere – that taking the 'rogue' took 'two or three days space'. If so, he was at liberty for some time.

Identified 'straightaway' by Richard Miles as 'the very man That did the crime', the role of Thomas Sergison as 'the Justice' is mentioned but not by name. The Ballad then provides a clear chronology and geography of Jacob's punishment, at least with the former regarding his execution:

> At Horsham Gallows he was hanged there
> The thirty first of August that same year
> And where he did the crime they took the pains
> To bring him back and hang him up in chains.

In this respect it adds to the general trend of the evidence that Jacob was hanged in the town where he had been imprisoned. The Ballad then ended in standard form as a morality tale – verses that, not surprisingly, the Victorian antiquarians were keen to reproduce.[107] On the gibbet, it was hoped that Jacob

> might be seen by all that passed by
> I wish all people who will cast an eye
> It is a dismal sight for to behold
> Enough to make a heart of stone run cold.

As if this was not blatant enough, the message was spelt out with a clear Christian message:

> So to conclude I hope you will take care
> And of all wilful sin I pray beware
> Let's serve the Lord with all our might
> And he will guard us day and night.

The history of gibbeting in the later early modern to modern period strongly suggests that its deterrent function largely failed to work in the popular imagination. It has been suggested that the verses of the 'Ballad of Jacob Harris' 'reveal some human sympathy for Harris' because of the two lines relating to the sight of his gibbeted body.[108] Beyond these, it is hard to make a definitive case that Jacob was being presented as a folk hero *just yet*. Although the word 'rogue' possessed an element of ambiguity in the eighteenth century, this was far less the case than has developed in the twentieth century and beyond. Jacob is presented in the Ballad largely as the outsider, and Miles as part of the locality and an innocent victim.

## The principal players and summary

What happened in the years and decades beyond the press reporting, the coroner's report, the trial, the hanging and the gibbeting, and the Ballad, has been lost from the archive – if records ever existed. It can, however, be put in the category of 'unknown knowns' that the site of the gibbeting developed as a special space and place. The meanings associated with it and the evolution of the site will be explored chronologically as this study progresses. It will be helpful here to pause and to summarise the 'knowable', the 'unknowable' and those in between when considering the contemporary archive and the misdeeds of Jacob Harris.

The first and most important point is that although the triple murders were not written about for over a century – indeed not until the 1850s – they were briefly a sensation not just locally but nationally in the year they happened. It remains that a triple murder, and one that was massively blood-soaked, had immense newsworthiness. The makings of a bureaucratic structure to deal with the administration of justice (and the recording of baptisms, marriages and burials) and the relative closeness of London (around fifty miles), even with the atrocious roads of Sussex, meant that within a week of the crime being committed it was reported in the *London Evening Post*, and from there often plagiarised, word for word, by other newspapers within and beyond the capital.[109]

Before the trial, the details of the murders were widely disseminated in the London and then provincial press. These reports were followed by details of the gibbeting, starting with the *London Evening Post*, which had provided the most detailed and sustained coverage of the murders. It reported only briefly on the conclusion of Jacob's punishment at 'Ditchelling Common in Sussex', reminding its readers that he had been 'James Jacob Daves, alias Harris, who was condemned at the last Assizes at Horsham, as we lately mentioned'.[109]

# Jacob Harris and the murders of 1734

By the very end of August, reporting came to an end, and the murders and the gibbeting were to receive no more printed attention until the mid-nineteenth century. At the time, a score of papers had, however, covered the story from the point at which Jacob Harris was still loose through to his ignoble hanging in chains on Ditchling Common. The story had enough gore and intrigue to merit such intensive coverage. For more than the next hundred years, its memory would be preserved essentially only at a local level. While the press played its role in making the story (in)famous, it was local knowledge, I will suggest, rather than the publicity generated, that allowed Jacob to be located and caught so quickly.

The next chapter will be devoted to Jacob Harris. Here, it is important to summarise what we know about the other key players in the 1734 narrative beyond those already outlined: the initial chronicler of the murders, John Stapley, and Thomas Sergison and John Oliver whose role the diarist recorded. Beyond Sergison, the most important figure in the prosecution of Jacob Harris was John Michell, one of the two coroners for Sussex at the time. Michell dealt with the east of the county. The assizes he oversaw alternated between Lewes and Horsham, and were held at least twice a year. Jacob Harris thus was 'fortunate' that he only had to wait a few months before his trial languishing in Horsham gaol, considering the conditions there. Little is known of Michell even though he was elected to the role of coroner as early as 1710. The editor of the *East Sussex Coroners' Records* notes that 'Michell's last surviving inquest is of 30 May 1734' – that is, of Jacob Harris – but he adds that 'he continued to attend assizes until 2 August 1735'.[110]

Much more is known of the two Justices who judged the trial on 12 August 1734, Sir Edward Probyn and Sir Robert Eyre. Coming from London, they had six cases brought before them that day. We have already mentioned Edward Saires, accused of breaking into a house and stealing from it, who was sentenced to be hanged but later reprieved. Thomas Martin was treated similarly for a similar crime. Elizabeth Walter of Cuckfield was accused of stealing a flaxen sheet, the punishment for which was to be 'burned in the hand' and paying her fees. William Moncriff's crime is not listed, but he was 'discharged paying his fees'. Samuel Burdges was 'convicted for an assault upon Jane Lambert, an infant with an intent to ravish her'. His punishment was precise: he 'must stand in and upon the pillory the next market day at Chichester for the space of one hour between 12 and 1 noon, and committed to the Common Gaol for three months and until he shall have paid the fine'.[111] Such was the worth of a young girl subject to sexual assault.

Jacob Harris was delivered before Sir Robert Eyre, the Chief Justice, whose verdict was 'wilful murder'.[112] As was the case with Michell, Eyre was coming to the end of his legal career. Born into a distinguished family of judges and members of Lincoln's Inn, Eyre was also a major figure in the governing of Britain, being MP for Salisbury from 1698 to 1710 and becoming the Solicitor General in 1708. His political career had its ups and downs and David Lemmings, in the *Oxford Dictionary of National Biography*, notes that he was accused of corruption. In '1729–30 he was one of the judges suspected of "screening" the prison gaolers who were being investigated by the House of Commons committee of inquiry into the state of prisons'. But despite the strong evidence against him, he was exonerated and continued his role as a circuit judge. The trial of Jacob Harris was to be one of his last, however, as he died the following year and was buried in Salisbury.[113]

Aside from her name, the sources tell us nothing about Dorothy Miles, and her servant left absolutely no trace in the record. It was to be the pattern of so many domestic workers. Through his will, Richard Miles provided some hints of his life. His first request was that, commending his soul 'into the hands of Almighty God ... and loving grace of Jesus Christ my only saviour', he be 'buried in a Christian and decent manner'.[114] As noted, Miles and his wife were buried in Wivelsfield churchyard, though it has not been possible to locate any marked graves for them.[115] The second was financial – 'the sum of Twenty One Pounds of lawful money', which was to be given to his 'first born son Thomas Page'. He was also to inherit 'all my wearing apparell'. The remainder of his moneys, goods and chattels were to be distributed to his 'loving Sister Mary Cranfield to be duly paid during her natural life', and for anything that remained after her demise to be divided between 'Thomas Page, Mary Page, John Page, William Page and Richard Page', his children. That they all had the surname Page shows that Miles had indeed changed his name.[116]

The will does not suggest that Miles was especially wealthy (just a few thousand pounds in twentieth-century terms), unless a much larger, undisclosed sum was going to his sister, which seems unlikely. It was to be executed by his 'Trusty friends', Richard Tanner and John Mill, both local to the area and the latter described as a 'Yeoman'.[117] Miles, we have emphasised, had close local connections, but why he changed his name is somewhat curious. That leaves Jacob Harris, and we will close with a source within a source that provides an intriguing glimpse into our anti-hero. *Walker's Weekly Penny Journal* was one of many that came and went in the first half of the eighteenth century. Only a couple of copies, both dating to 1735, survive.[118] Thanks, however, to a notification in the *Daily Journal* (17 August 1734), we learn much of this new publication, its contents and approach:

> This Journal contains two Sheets of fine Crown Paper, curiously printed in Folio ... one Sheet of which is a Compleat Collection of State Trials, and Proceedings on High Treason, Murder, Blasphemy, Rapes, Libels, Heresy, Coining, and other Offences, from the Reign of King Richard II down to the Present Time. The other Sheet always consists of a Letter of Entertainment from the Spectators, Guardians, Tatlers ... and Original Poems, Epigrams, and pleasant and jocole Tales; with the earliest Accounts of the most authentic News, both Foreign and Domestick.[119]

The paper, its printer, a Mr Robert Walker of Turn-again-Lane near Fleet Street, proclaimed, 'will be of great advantage to all Coffee-houses, Ale-houses, and Barbers'. Ingenuously, Walker claimed that the two sheets 'will employ two of their Customers at once with the Pleasure of Reading'.[120] What is significant is that Mr Walker, introducing the fifth number of his 'Weekly Penny Journal', did so by mentioning only its coverage of 'THE TRIAL OF DAVES, a Jew, for the Murder of Richard Miles, his Wife, and Maid Servant, at Ditchelling in Sussex, who was condemned at the Assizes last Tuesday at Horsham, for the County of Sussex; and who is to be hanged in Chains at Ditchelling Common'.[121] It is, like all our sources, both enticing in its contents and frustrating – no copies of it survive for 1734, and this advert is the only fragment of its content that year. That the advertisement used only this brief description of the trial as an example of content to lure new subscribers ('half the Price, tho' double the Quantity, of another Journal') is an indication of the contemporary power of the story and indeed its commercial worth.[122] It is also the first datable document that gives a description of Jacob as Jewish, intriguingly in this case with the English surname 'Daves'.

It was not only in recognising the murderer's Jewishness that Robert Walker was exceptional. Described as a 'distributor of patent medicines ... [he] was a prolific entrepreneur in print based in London' who continually published 'potentially libellous pamphlets' hostile to the government. In 1733 he was imprisoned briefly for print attacks on Whig Prime Minister Robert Walpole.[123] From there his interests became more commercial. He launched newspaper titles such as *Walker's Weekly Penny Journal* and, as indicated by his interest in Jacob Harris, trial reports. 'The bibliography of Walker's increasingly voluminous output is bewildering.'[124] Aside from his *Penny Journal*, in 1734 Walker started producing cheap editions of Shakespeare's works. This led to copyright court cases from other publishers from the later 1730s to the 1750s. Eventually

Walker's strategy of spinning multiple plates and surviving writs proved too much.[125] He fled England to avoid his creditors, returning to surrender himself to debtor's prison in 1755, and dying in 1761.[126] It is perhaps fitting that our triple murderer's Jewishness was outed by a critic of the establishment and no stranger to life behind bars.

What Walker had in common with so many of our principal players was that his origins were uncertain – the details of his 'parentage and upbringing remain the subject of speculation'.[127] At one end of our story we have figures such as Thomas Sergison MP, whose biography is well documented, and at the other the maidservant, who continues to remain nameless and placeless. Bettany Hughes has pointed out the 'inconvenient truth that women have always been 50% of the population, but only occupy around 0.5% of recorded history'.[128] Such gender distortion is amplified by class, here as domestic servant. In the middle are those on the margins of society whose changes of name and, in the case of Jacob Harris, multiple aliases reveal survival strategies in a tough world. Indeed, whether publisher, prosecutor, politician, publican or pedlar/smuggler, the lines between law abider and transgressor, or insider and outsider, were fluid and never easy to draw – until, as in the cases of Jacob Harris or the Hawkhust gang later, vicious murders of innocents were carried out. Even then it did not mean, locally at least, that Harris was regarded simply as an alien 'rogue'.

# 2

# Folklore and naming: in search of Jacob Harris

## Folklore: from the gibbeting to the body of Jacob Harris

The triple murder carried out by Jacob Harris was a remarkable crime which caused, even in the violent world of eighteenth-century England, something of a sensation. Even so, after the gibbeting the memory of it soon became obscure in the written archive. It was kept alive only in the local world of mid-Sussex through local/family memory, the site of the gibbet and the 'Ballad of Jacob Harris'. It was later to be rediscovered by Victorian antiquarians and others, achieving national prominence again. Establishing 'fact' from 'fiction' proves elusive with the 'hard' contemporary evidence, revealing the fragility, uncertainty and power relations of the archive, which has needed as much care as evaluating later folklore and memory. The latter are all we have to fill in the missing elements of the story, even if they add to our understanding of the emotional history of the crimes. It is still the case that the complex processes of transmission are reflected in huge chronological gaps: the first written 'proof' of the naming of Jacob's Post (the gibbet site) is close to ninety years after the gibbeting; the first full surviving printed version of the Ballad was published two hundred years after it was originally constructed; and when the story moves to the places of the murderer's hiding, there are no archival sources: the first reference to it is in the years before the bicentenary of the murders in 1934. In spite of the remaining absences, uncertainties and 'unknowables', the weaving together of both archive and memory sources creates a fascinating mosaic of everyday countryside life in the eighteenth century, which this chapter will explore.

If Jacob Harris was a smuggler, his dealing in contraband would have made him a useful person to know. He seems to have been even more handy (literally so) as a dead body, first as a spectacle and then as a source of magic and medicine. We are moving here from written documentation, no matter how problematic, to folklore and local memory and to the world of superstition and the persistence of paganism. If we do not know for certain where Jacob Harris was born and brought up, he had, in death, found a permanent and welcoming home. That a Jew, uniquely, should achieve such posthumous status despite – or even because of – his horrendous crimes will need some explanation.

The Sheriff's Cravings for 1734, which included the expenses relating to 'the excurson of Hirshals [sic] Harris for the murder of 3', including his gibbeting, is the last *contemporary* document on the crime. It was submitted by Sussex coroner John Michell on 3 July 1735 and approved to be paid in full by Prime Minister Robert Walpole a week later.[1] Remarkably, there are no further mentions in archives or printed material for the remaining years of the eighteenth century and decades beyond about the bloody events on Ditchling Common.

This silence is even more surprising given the continuing societal interest in crime at its most bloody and brutal. In terms of writing local history, there was neither interest nor knowledge of the murders. Dr William Burrell, whose vast archive at the British Library was collected for an 'Intended History of Sussex', while containing material and jottings on almost every subject,[2] did not include Jacob Harris. There were notes on Ditchling, including the Common, mainly on property ownership (especially the Manor) and the architecture of the church, and brief reference to the Sergison family in relation to Cuckfield.[3] Intriguingly, covering the 'monuments of Sussex', Burrell *did* examine the register of baptisms, marriages and burials at Wivelsfield. He noted down selected names before and after Richard and Elizabeth Miles but failed to mention the couple who were buried there on 1 June 1734.[4] Clearly, their entry and unusual status as 'murdered' was not something that he considered of any particular significance. Burrell died in 1796 before he could write his magnum opus, but the material he gathered informed the early published histories of the county. The most prominent of these were by Mark Antony Lower in 1831 and Thomas Horsfield in 1835. Both covered the villages of Ditchling and Wivelsfield but also made no mention of Jacob Harris.[5] This reflects the fact that by the 1830s, outside the locality knowledge of the murders was obscure, even in the wider county in which the crimes took place, or, like Burrell, they did not consider it at this stage to be the making of 'proper' history.

In 1870 an updated 'compedious' history of Sussex was published by Lower. It again covered Ditchling and this time *did* include a paragraph on the events of May 1734, referencing the 'remarkable tragedy [that] occurred in this parish

[when] Jacob Harris, a Jew pedlar, committed a very barbarous murder' on the Common. The brief details were taken from the two articles referencing the crime in the *Sussex Archaeological Collections*, which had appeared in the two decades before the new edition of Lower's history was published, supplemented by the brief appearance in *Notes and Queries*.[6] Crude and racialised as they were, the murders and gibbeting of Jacob Harris were now established 'facts' for Victorian antiquarians and, from them, for wider society – first the literate middle classes and then wider society through leisure pursuits and visits to the scene of the crime.

If history writing about Jacob Harris was slow in coming, it has been suggested in terms of implementing criminal justice that 'The gibbeting of John Breads [a butcher who mistakenly murdered a man in Rye, taking him for his foe, some fifty miles away] may have been inspired by that of Jacob Harris eight years earlier.'[7] In fact, gibbeting was relatively common and required no Sussex inspiration in the case of Breads. For the 1730s in England and Wales there were around fifty 'hangings in chains' and in the counties of Sussex, Essex, Gloucestershire and Hampshire between 'five or six gibbetings sometimes occurred within a decade'.[8] Indeed, it was noted by antiquarian Lewis Ackerman in the county magazine that 'Sussex had its [fair] share of gibbets'.[9] While such events were sufficiently unusual to mean local adjustment and innovation, there was no legal or performative precedence in the case of Jacob Harris, which, alongside the remoteness of where his crimes were committed, may have led to amnesia beyond the specific locality. As Ackermann noted, 'In the eighteenth and early nineteenth centuries, the gibbet, that stark, clanking emblem of death, was a common sight on the hill-tops and cross roads of England.'[10] In contrast, the gibbet on Ditchling Common, being on neither hilltop nor crossroads, was less visible in the landscape. To know what happened to the memory of the murders from 1735 to over a century later, we will have to turn to folk legend and local memory.

After Jacob's hanging in chains, there is no doubt that the site of the gibbeting was visited and preserved: it was a special, liminal place. As Sarah Tarlow asks, more generally: 'what kind of a thing is a gibbeted body? Is it a person? Or is it a thing?'[11]

The cage in which he was hanged typically would have been made locally by a blacksmith and tailored to fit his frame – it was one of the precise costings in the Sheriff's Cravings.[12] Over the following years his body would have decomposed, the deterioration hastened, as with other gibbetings, by birds and other wild animals eating Jacob's flesh and taking away his bones. The gibbet cage itself and the post would be vulnerable as they could be repurposed as scrap. Sometimes the cadaver would be dipped in boiling pitch to ensure it remained as a longer lasting warning and to act as a deterrent to those that wanted to touch the body.[13] This does not seem to have happened with Jacob. Depending on the quality of the cage and the gibbet not collapsing or the body being removed, it was normally the case that the bones of the lower body would fall through the cage, eventually leaving only the cranium. This is what happened with John Breads in Rye, whose skull with the original iron cage is still macabrely displayed in the town hall.[14] While the source for it is incomplete and uncertain, this pattern of skeleton collapse seems to have been what happened with Jacob Harris.

In 1883, the *Mid-Sussex Times*, founded two years earlier and in which the story of the Ditchling Common murders would continue to feature regularly, carried a brief history of the 'One O'Clock' farm which was located less than a mile away from the site of Jacob's gibbet. It was an extract from a publication called *Five Generations of a Mid-Sussex Family* which, like the original Ballad, sadly seems lost to posterity.[15] The particular episode referenced an event which occurred around the 1750s. It related to a smallpox outbreak and a young couple taking refuge at the farm while affected by this terrible and horribly infectious disease. Remarkably, the newlyweds were cured, it was claimed, by consuming copious quantities of turnips. The narrator breaks off from this peculiar medical success to inform the reader that close by was the gibbet post holding Jacob's cage, 'which, by the way, at that time held its ghastly-looking head in all its glory'.[16] The 'One O'Clock' farm, which had pioneered the cultivation of turnips, was at the heart of this family history, and it is thus very likely that the proximity of the gibbet would have been regularly and, at least for the young, traumatically experienced by its members as an everyday occurrence and thereafter remaining in family mythology.

In the first volume of the *Folk Lore Record* in 1878, Charlotte Latham relayed 'Some West Sussex Superstitions', and how the belief in magic persisted well into the nineteenth century. Rather than fully distance herself from them, she recalled her childhood some thirty-five years earlier, and a gibbet on the road to Brighton:

> it was an object of great terror to me in my youthful days; and the dread of seeing it and hearing my nurse repeat her oft-told tale of the murderer who had been hung on it in chains, and how he had been seen swinging on a windy night and heard rattling his irons, made the prospect of a visit to the sea-side, which involved the sight of the gallows, anything but pleasurable.[17]

Similarly, the grotesque remnants of Jacob when possibly only his head was still in the cage would no doubt have become ingrained in memory, especially for those living so close to the site or passing it on a daily basis. Ackermann was allowing himself artistic licence, but his description of the triple murderer 'clank[ing] as he swung in his iron shroud at the end of the chain' is likely to have been accurate.[18] It remains that the legends associated with the gibbet on Ditchling Common are even less precise in chronology and detail than those relating to the 'One O'Clock' farm, subject to distortion and invention by Victorian antiquarians and folklorists. Nonetheless, they still deserve to be given due (if careful) consideration both in what they reveal about their subject matter and an ongoing engagement with Jacob Harris.

We have already encountered the Reverend Edward Turner and his doctoring of the Stapley diary, reproduced in *Sussex Archaeological Collections* in 1866. Nevertheless, it *is* true that Turner had deep family roots in Ditchling and he recalled an 'excellent old lady, and an aunt of my mother, who lived in her single, married, and afterwards widowed state, for upwards of eighty years, at no great distance' from the gibbet post. 'All gibbets', Turner noted, 'are imagined to possess a power of enchantment.' That on Ditchling Common, according to the Reverend, had a 'peculiar preventive virtue against aching teeth, a small piece of it carried in the pocket being an effectual remedy against that racking disorder'. His great-aunt 'was accustomed to expatiate largely on its efficacy' and would not fail to have it on her person. The Reverend Turner clearly had no time for this belief in magic other than to dismiss such superstition by mocking that she continued to have the gibbet fragment 'though she had long ceased to have a tooth remaining in her jaws'.[19]

Henry Cheal also had long family connections to Ditchling – one of his ancestors was a witness at Jacob Harris's trial. Cheal relayed a conversation held as 'recently as 1881' when a local doctor was 'called to a man who was in an epileptic fit'. He was told by a 'native of Newick' (a village some ten miles away), 'Ah! Sir, pity sure a lye, he 'and't a bit of Jacob's Poist in his pocket!' To emphasise his point to the incredulous doctor, the man added that 'people comes *moils* and *moils*, from round Ashdown Forest way, to get a bit of dat poisty'.[20] This testimony was, in fact, borrowed from local physician, Thomas Blaker, in his pamphlet extolling the virtues of Burgess Hill (a mile from Wivelsfield) as a 'health resort', which was published in 1883. Responding to such advice on how to avoid falling 'wiv these yer fits' from this 'native', Blaker sardonically tells his readers: 'So we live and learn.'[21] While far from unique in this respect, Jacob's Post does seem to have been considered especially

JACOB'S POST.
*(On Ditchling Common.)*

**Figure 3** Remnants of the gibbet post, illustration from Thomas Blaker, *Burgess Hill as a Health Resort* (1883)

beneficial in the world of folk medicine, having 'the miraculous property of preventing ague, neuralgia and other ailments in those who carried a splinter of its wood in their pockets'.[22]

The gibbeted body, especially the 'dead man's hand', was also meant to possess magical powers, including for women struggling to become pregnant.[23] It has been claimed that this was true for the body of Jacob Harris: 'women who were barren went to the corpse when still hung at Ditchling and after holding its hand would become fertile'.[24] Such precise, if disturbing, bodily intimacy served wider purposes: Charlotte Latham claimed that the 'revolting remedy' of passing the hand of such a corpse several times over the swollen part was 'still resorted to for the cure of wens or goitre in the throat'.[25] There is every possibility that such practices took place with the cadaver of Jacob Harris. In fact the health problems caused by such close contact with the dead body was one of the major reasons why gibbeting was formally abandoned in the Anatomy Act of 1832. Instead, this Act allowed for the bodies of those executed to be used more directly and 'scientifically' for medical purposes. Jacob Harris was 'lucky' in that, unlike Jewish criminals at the end of the eighteenth century, surgeons did not seek out his 'racially' different body for special treatment.

What *is* certain in our case is that the site became known and recognised as Jacob's Post some time in the eighteenth century – Cheal claimed that it was known as such 'since the crime [was committed]'.[26] There were newspaper references to it in 1823 and to a proposed road the year following.[27] To work effectively, such casual references assumed knowledge of where exactly the site was located and the name must therefore have been in common usage for some time before the 1820s – the specific naming revealing its local importance.

It has been suggested that 'the criminal hung in chains was written enduringly into the landscape. His name often became inalienable from the place of his gibbet, and his particular crime and fate was remembered through the erection of what was, effectively, a monument.'[28] Jacob's Post fits that model perfectly. In 1901, the year that brought the Victorian era to an end, Henry Cheal published his history of Ditchling. Organist of the parish church there, he used the extensive diaries of the yeoman Thomas Marchant of the neighbouring mid-Sussex village of Hurstpierpoint to outline the everyday life of Ditchling. Cheal reproduced Marchant's entry for 16 July 1721: 'My wife and I at Ditchling to see my cousin Nicholas Marchant's widow, who is ill. We were at church and afterwards at my Aunt Turner's. Mr. Porter of Chailey preacht.'[29]

This diary usage illustrated what Cheal believed was the peace and harmony of the village and its surrounds, part of a wider absence of 'atrocious crimes and tragedies' in the 'early annals of Sussex history'. The one exception he acknowledged to this otherwise bucolic world with the local Anglican place of worship at its heart was 'one of the most terrible and dastardly crimes which have ever taken place in this county'. It happened in the Royal Oak Inn, 'on the northern borders of Ditchling Common, an open, dreary, and desolate waste, infested with highwaymen and footpads'. Cheal then outlined the three murders carried out by Jacob Harris, 'a Jew pedlar', and how his 'ghastly gibbet ... was exhibited as a warning to all evil doers'.[30]

Jacob Harris was thus presented by Cheal, following the writings of those in the Sussex Archaeological Society, as what anthropologist Mary Douglas famously described as 'matter out of place'.[31] For Cheal, if Marchant's world of church and the Christian virtue of visiting sick relatives was the epitome of cleanliness and what Douglas would classify as the necessity of order, Jacob Harris and his 'Jewishness' by necessity had to be presented as *other* to Ditchling's past, and a disruptive and destructive alien force. Cheal's inclusion of Jacob as the ultimate outsider thus enhanced, rather than undermined, his narrative of Ditchling and the village's inner purity: 'dirt is that which must not be included if a pattern is to be maintained'.[32] 'Dirt', however, Douglas insists, is a 'relative idea'.[33] Concepts of it are mutable, and there are things, whether they be food, material culture or ritual, that are ambiguous.[34] Jacob Harris could be dealt with easily by Victorian moralisers and their descendants as an anomaly, 'a Jew pedlar' perpetrator responsible for 'one of the most atrocious crimes ever committed' on 'Sussex soil', who carried out 'the wholesale extermination of a household': he was an exception that proved the rule of innocence and harmony in a county allegedly free from the stains of violent perversity.[35] What worried them was that Jacob was remembered with some degree of affection and was seen as part of – and not apart from – the local world.

A few years after Cheal's history of Ditchling was written, the prolific travel writer, E. V. Lucas, reflected on the 1734 murders. Lucas had a strong attachment to Sussex, including the place of the crimes, recalling later in his life visiting that location in Ditchling Common 'when I was a child'.[36] In his *Highways and Byways in Sussex* (1904), Lucas described Jacob Harris as a 'Jew pedlar of astonishing turpitude'.[37] Just as Cheal had used an eighteenth-century Sussex diarist as a foil to Jacob Harris, so Lucas used the autobiographical writings of John Burgess of Ditchling to show its *true* character. In the 1780s Burgess's diary described a world of cricket matches, dinners of 'boiled Beef, Leg of Lamb and plum Pudden', and '3 or 4 hours with some friends in Conversation upon Moral and religious Subjects'.[38]

What annoyed Lucas was the naming of the remains of the gibbet in Ditchling Common as '*Jacob's* post [my emphasis]'. In this respect, Jacob's 'name has in this familiar connection a popular and almost an endearing sound'.[39] A few decades later, another author had to warn his readers that this Jacob was 'not a biblical figure as might be thought [but] a Jewish pedlar'.[40] Lucas was not mistaken – as a folk legend, the memory of Jacob Harris was warmly evoked around mid-Sussex. Furthermore, the place of his gibbeting was a meaningful feature of the local landscape linked to medical cures and benevolent magic. As Sarah Tarlow and Zoe Dyndor argue more generally, 'The gibbet functioned as a mnemonic: the massive crowds and carnival at the occasion of its erection served to make the occasion unforgettable in local memory.'[41] What was unusual in the case of Jacob Harris is that the gibbet site was not his only lasting memorial.

## Transmitting the 'Ballad of Jacob Harris'

If the exact dating of the Ballad is extremely likely to be 1734, what *is* certain is that it was, remarkably, responsible for the extensive details of the murders being preserved in local culture for the centuries that followed. In that respect, its impact was mutually reinforced by the preservation of the gibbet site itself. The Ballad evoked an element of sympathy and empathy with the perpetrator, especially when juxtaposed with the naming of *Jacob's* Post. In a study of ballads and the 'emotional life of crime', it has been suggested that 'Audience imagination of criminal experience, for all its ambiguity, enabled a vicarious participation in deviant lives.'[42] There is an irony here in that Richard Miles gave the details which formed the basis of contemporary newspaper coverage, which in turn provided the substance of the Ballad. From these 'rude verses', it was Jacob Harris, rather than Miles, his first victim of throat cutting, who would be subsequently remembered through a process of 'common human feeling that bound the public observer to the inner experience of the criminal'.[43]

The Ballad, almost certainly produced (and probably performed) for the occasion of the gibbeting, was just as critical as Jacob's Post in the process of local remembering, and was at times inseparable from it with regard to place and space. In 1861, the then vicar of Ditchling, Thomas Hutchinson, in a random collection of historical 'facts' about the village, suggested that the memory of the 'Jew pedlar who committed a very barbarous murder' in Ditchling Common was 'kept alive in the neighbourhood ... by some rude verses still preserved among the people'.[44] As noted, five years earlier, R. W. Blencowe, leading light of the Sussex Archaeological Society, made the first reference in print to the Ballad in the popular journal *Notes and Queries*. Blencowe went further than Hutchinson and described them as *very* rude verses [my emphasis]'. He also emphasised that they were 'still preserved in the neighbourhood'.[45]

The proximity of Blencowe and Hutchinson to Ditchling Common may well have facilitated them gathering fragments of the Ballad from the local population, whether in oral or printed/written form. If so, it would fit to some extent the pattern identified by Vic Gammon in his study of folk song collecting in Sussex and Surrey. The collectors tended to be from the middle classes, with leisure on their side, and the singers were 'overwhelmingly from the labouring poor of the countryside'. It was, as he adds, therefore 'the meeting of two rather different social worlds'.[46] Where it differs is that neither Blencowe nor Hutchinson were interested in collecting folk music per se, hence their snobbish dismissal of the Ballad as 'rude' verses – that is, unsophisticated and vulgar. While Sussex was prime territory for folk song collectors, starting with John Broadwood and then his niece Lucy in the nineteenth century, the more obscure, middle parts of the county were mined less. Furthermore, the 'middle decades of the [eighteenth century were] something of a barren period for printed ballad investigation'. Nevertheless, with its 'stock phrases of broadside ballad makers and ... use of some commonplace verses', Vic Gammon is strongly of the view that the Ballad of 1734 is contemporary.[47] That the specific content and wording follows closely from the newspaper reports, especially the *London Evening Post*, adds weight to his conviction.[48] Yet how the Ballad as a whole was preserved beyond 1734 is open to speculation and provides a fascinating case study of transmission of this important genre of folk history.

There is an ongoing important debate about folk memory and whether it is kept alive through oral tradition or print culture. The expansion of the print marketplace in the eighteenth century undoubtably changed the balance, including the world of ballads. It has been suggested that cheap print allowed for the production of a 'great quantity of sad trash'. The more recent consensus, however, is that the binary between the primacy of 'oral or print' is unsatisfactory and that both were important and interrelated.[49] As Steve Roud suggests in his definitive *Folk Song in England* (2017), 'Oral/aural transmission has always been an extremely important component in folk traditions, but since the invention of printing, there has probably never been a purely "oral" tradition, even among the lower classes.'[50] As argued by Adam Fox, for the early modern period in England, where illiteracy was still common and close to the norm, those able to read would do so amongst family and groups of friends, revealing the interdependency of written and spoken stories in a variety of genres, whether secular or religious in content.[51]

The 'Ballad of Jacob Harris' almost certainly was not locally penned. It was part of the 'nexus of print, commerce and balladry' that had opportunistically appeared in the eighteenth century.[52] It is possible that some printed copies sold at the gibbeting of Jacob in 1734 were preserved, or that a version was written down by hand and displayed in the Royal Oak itself – this was probably the case with the pub in the twentieth century. A good case could be made, however, that oral/aural transmission played an important role, leading to the 'various versions' that are apparent in the full reproductions appearing around the bicentenary of the murders, and then later when recorded by Sussex folk singer Gordon Hall and in print within other local sources.[53]

Dick Morley, in his memoir and history of Ditchling, *No Ordinary Place*, goes to the other extreme from Blencowe and Hutchinson, who dismissed the literary qualities of the Ballad, and suggests it is 'remarkably reminiscent of Chaucer. I see it as belonging more to the fourteenth century than to the eighteenth.' Although his chronological conjecture is suspect and he is more than generous about the verses, with their excruciating and laboured rhyming, Morley is right in arguing that to be appreciated 'it needs to be spoken rather than read',[54] and, one might add, performed. He is also close to the truth when he suggests that 'the gruesome details of the triple murder were soon in print and retailed by the eighteenth century equivalent of the tabloid press'.[55] In fact, the new penny evening presses of the eighteenth century were not far removed from more modern 'yellow journalism', and provided the 'copy' for the Ballads and their subsequent afterlife as folk song.

The only hint we have of how that oral/aural transmission occurred in relation to our Ballad is through the remarkable career of Sussex folk singer, Gordon Hall (1932–2000). Described as 'one of the finest traditional folk singers of the late twentieth century', Hall was 'a huge man both physically and in personality', a 'wonderful singer and [a] monumental man [who] broke cars for a living'.[56] On the surface, the model of an oral tradition following the initial printing of the Ballad seems extremely convincing, and not simply because Blencowe and Hutchinson, using mid-nineteenth-century local knowledge, suggested that this was indeed the model of transmission. That it was Gordon Hall who preserved the content of the Ballad appears to support the 'oral transmission' model further. As Roud further suggests, the tunes of folk ballads were more variable and words could be made to fit according to the repertoire and choice of the performer: 'in the folk sphere … there is often a very weak connection between text and tune'.[57]

Although born in south London, Hall had strong Sussex roots, being schooled in Horsham, the town of Jacob Harris's imprisonment and probably the place of his hanging. Gordon Hall travelled widely but lived most of his adolescent and adult life in the county.[58] Significantly, both his mother and maternal grandmother came from Wivelsfield and it was from them, directly or indirectly, that he became aware of many local folk songs. Asked in a radio interview in 1991 by friend and fellow folk aficionado and collector, Vic Smith, how he learned the huge range of ballads in his repertoire, Gordon Hall gently retorted that 'You don't learn them, old son, when you've been brought up like I have – you absorb them', and that it was in large measure through his mother, Mabs. Hall then outlined how when confronted with the printed words of one of the folk songs Mabs performed, 'it didn't mean a thing to her … Very often, she wouldn' realise it was the same thing as she had sung all her life'.[59]

Asked further by Vic Smith from whom Mabs had absorbed her songs, Hall responded that is was through his maternal grandmother. While Gordon 'was never lucky enough to meet' her, his grandmother was 'a wonderful woman [who] knew hundreds of songs'.[60] In a later and wonderfully chaotic, not fully sober, interview with Gwilym Davies and Ray Driscoll for the British Library's sound archive, Gordon Hall described his grandmother as 'the witch of Wivelsfield' who was 'full of old wives' tales'.[61] His grandmother 'was completely illiterate', having to sign Mabs's birth certificate with a cross.[62] Against the model proposed by Adam Fox of a productive relationship between those who could read and those who could not, 'My grandmother would actually knock a book out of my mother's hand. She wouldn't allow her to read. This was the work of the devil – books!'[63]

All this might suggest the greater weight of the oral tradition in the transmission of the Ballad, especially with Gordon's close family connection to Wivelsfield (his grandmother and mother lived at 'Cheel's cottage', a family name, as noted, with both contemporary and later connections to the story of Jacob Harris).[64] Nevertheless, it is also the case that, from the mid-1980s, Hall was carrying out his own research into Sussex folk songs. In 1991 he said: 'I want to find out as much as I can about every song I've ever *heard* and trying to delve into them. In the case of the big ballads, to try and find out how true they are to the living history [my emphasis].'[65] He then recorded over 200 songs in his own house, most of which have been made available through the 'Sussex Traditions: Folklife & Lore' website,[66] and others, including the 'Ballad of Jacob Hirsch', through the British Library Sound Archive.

Of the two versions of the Ballad printed in the 1930s, Gordon Hall's is closer to that of Horsham antiquarian William Albery, initially printed in the *Sussex County Magazine*, including the phrase 'his spleen to show't', the last word certainly not in common usage by the twentieth century.[67] Even then, Hall made some small changes and more significant amendments, singing that the murders took place 'In Wivelsfield by Ditchling Common side', referencing the *Royal Oak* alehouse and referring to Jacob Harris as a 'pedlar' and later as a 'chapman', none of which appear in any other printed version.[68] It was, as he said more generally in his performance of ballads, adding 'local knowledge'.[69] He also labelled the recording as a 'murder ballad [relating to] Jacob Harris (also known as Jacob Hirsch) a travelling peddler'. The use of 'Hirsch' suggests a knowledge of the murderer's background. Yet in the verses Hall deliberately refrained from referencing Jacob as a 'Jew rogue'. In this he follows Albery's version, in contrast to the 1934 reproduction in the *Mid-Sussex Times* which labels him as such.[70]

Returning to his maternal grandmother, Gordon Hall related that she 'knew hundreds of songs. But according to Mother, she would only sing snatches.'[71] Given the length of the 'Ballad of Jacob Harris/Hirsch', this suggests that if there was a local oral tradition of reciting the Ballad, it was likely to have been incomplete. The differences in the printed versions of the 1930s and again with Gordon Hall's rendition suggest at least interpretations that reflect later input. It seems likely, therefore, that while the verses had their origins in a contemporary broadside which was constructed mainly from newspaper reports and standard murder ballads, it thereafter had its own life – albeit one that did not vary much from the original. To summarise: it was probably performed at the gibbeting of Jacob Harris and survived locally through printed and handwritten versions and possibly oral tradition.

Gordon Hall had close and continuing connections to Horsham (his family lived in the same house occupied by the earlier Sussex folk singer and collector, Henry Burstow). It is more than feasible that Hall read the version of the Ballad reproduced by William Albery in his history of the town published just after the Second World War. Here, significantly, Albery reproduced the coroner's report which referred to 'Jacob Hirsch otherwise Harris'.[72] That Albery was the major source for Gordon Hall is given further credence as Albery, or his researcher, has mistranscribed 'Hirsch', which in the original legal document is 'Hirsh'.[73] Neatly, in respect of a Horsham linkage, Albery had ghostwritten the memoirs of Burstow.[74] Even so, Gordon Hall had given the Ballad some thought, adding important topographical and biographical details and filling in missing lines with emphasis especially on Wivelsfield and the Royal Oak itself. It is still not impossible, therefore, that he had heard the Ballad or verses from it sung to him by his mother, who in turn learned it from his grandmother. An alternative scenario was that the Ballad was not performed at all after 1734 until Gordon Hall recorded it some 220 years later, and it survived only through a variety of printed or written forms in the neighbourhood, including at the Royal Oak.

## Jacob Harris as fugitive from the law

The 'Ballad of Jacob Harris' provides a clear narrative of the murders and the gibbeting but tells us nothing of what happened in between. We know from Richard Miles's testimony that Jacob Harris escaped the crime scene on his horse, and from the diary of John Stapley we are told that he was caught some time later at Turner's Hill, a good twenty miles away. That is as far as our datable contemporary sources can take us. We are then confronted with folk memory that is geographically precise, to some extent persuasive, but ultimately unverifiable about where exactly he was caught and how. That the details have become part of the standard narrating of the story is important, but not necessarily proof of their accuracy. Some aspects are more fanciful than others. The topographical precision and contextualisation *is* compelling, but a degree of caution is still essential. The best that can be done here is, as elsewhere in these opening chapters, to provide an 'archaeology of knowledge', and as Michel Foucault insists, 'the questioning of the *document*'.[75] In the process we must again at least give a fair hearing to local folk memory.

Jacob's journey at dusk and through a rural landscape with appalling roads would not have been an easy one. It suggests a topographical familiarity and local belonging. In the absence of documentation of this aspect of the story, those confronting it have resorted to literary devices, none more so than local historian and folk song collector Ursula Ridley,[76] in her evocative history of West Hoathly (close to Turner's Hill) in *The Story of a Forest Village* (1971). Ridley is open about her methodology. Using wills, inquests and other contemporary legal documents and a remarkable knowledge of local property ownership, she aimed at 'using no facts which cannot be verified'. Ridley added that she 'thought it desirable at times to introduce conversations of a fanciful character between real persons for the sake of giving the feelings of a Wealden village at a particular time'.[77]

A chapter of her history of West Hoathly is devoted to Jacob Harris – it remains one of the longest treatments of the murders. Having given a somewhat racialised and extravagant description of the crime in which, having already attacked Miles and his servant, 'The Jew ran wildly into the low ceilinged room where he had often observed a heavy, ironbound money-chest', Jacob Harris killed Mrs Miles. Ridley continued that Jacob realised that the box was empty and fled on his horse.[78] While the order and execution of the murders is confused, Ridley was most probably accurate, through her spatial knowledge and the details of land and property ownership, in describing what was likely his journey from the Royal Oak. Jacob, she creatively imagined,

> found himself heading for the open moor round Haywards Heath. He rode through Lindfield in a frenzy. He left the highroad at Lyewood Common and rode down the steep hill past Jasper Wheeler's house at Burstowe Bridge, and up to Hamingden where the road twists twice … The long arms of the mill at Whitestone stood out against the dark sky. He rode along the windy ridge above Grovelands and Stephen Sawyer's land. Turning left at the Image Cross and passing Mr Sawyer's tannery at Hoathly Hill. This was John Stoner's new shop.

Jacob's initial journey was now nearly complete: he 'hurried round the bend at Hell's Corner' and stopped at the top of the hill. 'He had reached that wide-roofed haunt of smugglers, pedlars, farmers, artizans, the Cat Inn.'[79]

From there, Jacob gets wind that the Riding Officers are in close pursuit and he moves on, rejecting the Three Tuns pub because the landlord 'was no friend of smugglers or those connected to them', but he reaches Selsfield Common and with his by now limping horse knocks at Selsfield House in Turner's Hill, where he knew the owners, Mr and Mrs Stoner. The Riding Officers have now caught up with Jacob and his hosts explain away his horse and hide him on a secret ledge in the chimney of their big fireplace. Wet from the rain, the officers demand that the fire is lit so their uniforms could dry – on cue, Jacob falls to the bottom of the fire. 'Rendered unconscious by the smoke, Jacob had fallen at his pursuers' feet.'[80]

There is no doubt that Ridley knew her local material well and she performs this precisely in her narration by slipping in who owned or lived in each particular building in the vicinity to give it a human touch, adding to her vivacious storytelling.[81] As with the Reverend Turner, however, the power of archive ownership is also at work here. She and then her descendants had possession of West Hoathly's ancient records which recorded ownership of property.[82] The manorial chest she had inherited was largely made up of centuries-old legal documentation, but it also included more modern material. Within it was 'The Story of a Murder', which was probably written by the vicar of the church in West Hoathly, the Reverend Dr C. Valentine, 'some time in the late 1940s'. Ridley took most of the details and the overall story from this earlier text, which presents Jacob Harris in a more favourable way than she was to do.[83]

Beyond the characters who are introduced and how they relate to the buildings of the locality (including the Cat Inn), the manorial chest, sold by the Ridley family to the West Sussex Record Office in 2023, does not contain particular archive material on Jacob Harris. It remains unknown whether Valentine and Ridley were relying on folk memory for details of his attempts to escape justice. They were not, however, the first to describe this epic journey and episode in the story of Jacob Harris. While all the contemporary documentation possessed a performative nature, right back to the coroner's report and its standard line that Jacob was 'possessed by the Devil',[84] from the twentieth century the representations of the crimes rely more and more on literary imagination. When combined with detailed research, as with Valentine and Ridley, the reader is at least brought into a closer understanding of the human dimension of these shocking crimes.

Some short time before the bicentenary, probably in the late 1920s or early 1930s, a local newspaper piece by 'South Saxon' was published devoted to 'Jacob's toothache post'. Undated and without indication of source, the cutting is among the research papers of David Spector, collected in his quest during the late twentieth century to find out more about Jacob Harris and Sussex Jewry as a whole. The article was designed for the leisure motorist and provided a neat sketch map so that the driver could follow Jacob's journey by car. As will emerge, from the late nineteenth century onwards Jacob's Post became a well-known stopping place for cyclists, motor clubs and motorbike riders as well as meeting place for hunts and social groups. South Saxon, however, was the only one to provide a complete Jacob Harris murder tour – however ethically dubious.[85]

The route South Saxon picked for Jacob is similar if not identical to that chosen by Ursula Ridley – from the Royal Oak through Wivelsfield, then Haywards Heath to Lindfield, and from there to West Hoathly via Balcome Ardingly. South Saxon, however, had more empathy with regard to the physical and emotional challenges facing Jacob in his quest for freedom:

> Haywards Heath, now so new and suburban, was then as its name implies just a heath; Lindfield a timbered village centred around an early English church, a place for a murderer to hurry through as quickly as possible.
>
> Northwards again along what is now the B2028 but then but a muddy track beneath the giant oaks of near impassible Sussex. With few houses to pass and only isolated farms Jacob must have got his nerve back as he rode and stumbled through the difficult country getting farther and farther away from the scene.

South Saxon realised that by the time Jacob Harris had reached the Cat Inn, he would have been totally exhausted. As with Ridley, South Saxon took the narrative from the Cat Inn to nearby Selsfield House, where he remains just one small step ahead of the militia. Where it differs is in the journalist's awareness that the episode involving the smoking fire with Jacob falling 'coughing from his hiding place at their feet' was a fictional embellishment. To emphasise the point, South Saxon suggests that things from the Cat Inn onwards take 'a whimsical turn'.[86]

What then are we to make of this part of our story? Turner's Hill is tiny today, with a population of fewer than 2,000, and was much smaller in the early eighteenth century. While subsequently expanded, Selsfield House was one of the larger houses in the village and was also closest to the Cat Inn – and we know that Turner's Hill was the place he was brought back from. There *is* a large and impressive fireplace where Jacob could easily have hidden out of sight,[87] though the falling at the feet of his pursuers is too neat an ending to his escape journey. It also fits a trope of popular fiction where the criminal hides up a chimney and comes – one way or another – to a sticky end. Finding refuge in the Cat Inn – a pub known to be a safe space for smugglers – makes sense, as does, in increasing desperation, the hiding in a private house owned by some-one likely to be known by the murderer. The earliest written evidence of Jacob's stay at the Cat Inn and Selsfield House is, however, from the 1920s or 1930s, even if this was from a 'story handed down over the years'.[88]

Aside from the fanciful damp Riding Officers with their 'wet uniforms steam-ing',[89] it seems likely that the journey described by first South Saxon and then Ursula Ridley was close enough to the essence of what happened in the few days Jacob was at liberty after the murders. Even then, for narrative impact the story is condensed into a framework of roughly twelve hours – from dusk until dawn. We know that it took several days to find Jacob Harris and bring him back to Ditchling Common. He thus may well have been in either the Cat Inn or Selsfield House for some time before those searching caught up with him. He was not to know that Richard Miles had survived long enough to identify him, which might explain his tardiness in leaving Sussex completely.

**Figure 4** Selsfield House, where Jacob Harris was caught

**Figure 5** The fireplace in Selsfield House where Jacob Harris allegedly hid

Ultimately, those last days of Jacob's freedom must remain speculative, and the historian is thus reliant on the local knowledge and imagination of South Saxon, the Reverend Valentine and Ursula Ridley. It is possible that, frustratingly as ever, there is contemporary archive material that has survived but is not available, but this is unlikely. It would still be surprising if South Saxon was the first to put down on paper this part of the Jacob Harris storyline, which has now become standard in its narration, but no earlier mentions have been located, including in the West Hoathly Local History Archive. The connection to the Cat Inn and then Selsfield House (which is one of the places meant to be haunted by Jacob Harris) *could* conceivably be remembered through local folk memory alone. More likely is the existence of some lost or inaccessible documentation that, as with the Ballad, allowed a mixture of oral and written sources to enable its continued transmission for close to two centuries. Alternatively, they could be pure fiction – understandable in the case of the Cat Inn, which could use an invented heritage for commercial gain, but less convincing with Selsfield House and the hamlet where we know Jacob was taken.

## Folklore and naming: in search of Jacob Harris

After 1945, West Hoathly and Turner's Hill became rivals with Ditchling in storytelling about Jacob Harris, adding interest but also creating confusion about details. All in all, it seems most likely that both the Cat Inn and Selsfield House were Jacob's places of asylum having fled the scene of his crimes, as advanced by South Saxon, Valentine and Ridley. Of these three mid-twentieth-century versions, Valentine is the exception in one important respect. To the other two, Jacob Harris was undoubtedly a 'Jewish pedlar' – though only Ridley makes something of this identity, and generally in a negative way. It will be to this part of his identity, using both the contemporary documentation and folklore, that we will turn to complete this chapter. How has Jacob Harris been remembered for his Jewishness?

## Jacob's Post, the third space and Jewishness

We have seen that the gibbet post (or what purported to be it) was revered. It was preserved through the nineteenth century and beyond, showing the local attachment to it. In his remarkable cultural history of Rye, John Breads and his gibbeting in 1743, Paul Monod suggests that Jacob Harris would not have 'been exposed on a gibbet if he had not been a Jew'.[90] For all their prejudices expressed through crass terminology, the Georgian courts were not biased in their treatment either of victims or perpetrators because of their Jewishness, or at least not until the late eighteenth century. It is thus not clear that, as Monod continues, Jacob Harris was 'the ultimate outsider in a rural, settled, Christian environment'.[91] This *is* certainly how the Victorian and Edwardian commentators such as Turner, Cheal, Lucas and others presented him, but it is not necessarily the case for how Jacob's contemporaries in mid-Sussex viewed him either in 1734 or later. Regarding Jacob as 'matter out of place' perhaps reveals more about these later writers than it does about the time they described. Yet rather than being a binary place defined by Christian self and Jewish other as so viciously demarcated by Lucas and others, we might better see Jacob's Post as what Homi Bhabha describes as the 'third space'.

Those around Jacob Harris were at least nominally Christian, and Jacob Harris was in some ways Jewish. Such labels did not, however, stop everyday interaction. Furthermore, the gibbet space went beyond these loose categorisations, embracing also forms of paganism in a 'dynamic process of hybridity'. To Bhabha, 'the importance of hybridity is not to trace two original moments from which the third emerges, rather hybridity ... is the "third space" which enables other positions to emerge. This third space displaces the histories that

65

constitute it.' Jacob Harris, as remembered and commemorated through Jacob's Post, meets this concept, giving 'rise to something different, something new and unrecognisable, a new area of negotiation of meaning and representation'.[92]

It was the very naming of his monument and the questioning of authority that upset those who saw Jacob as 'dirt' and were disappointed and irritated that he had become a folk hero. If the crime ballad superficially had a 'penitential framing [and] was informed with Christian assumptions about sin, conscience, and judgment', it has been suggested that 'the emotions invoked often had a distinctively secular bent'.[93] In the case of Jacob's body, the performance of the gibbeting and its afterlife, it is not so much secular as a 'something different' going beyond watertight categories of Christian, Jewish and pagan, secular and religious. As the nineteenth century progressed, and Jacob's Jewishness became a constant descriptor of the murderer, the belief in medical magic associated with the remains of the gibbet post did not fully diminish. Indeed, the belief in the ghostly, supernatural forces at work at the principal sites continues into the twenty-first century.[94] For all its messiness in what it meant, Jacob's Post remained a special place.

If this was true of acts of remembrance and folk memory, an element of Jewishness was not necessarily a barrier to local and national belonging in Jacob's lifetime. In exploring where Jacob and other Jews fitted in Georgian Britain, we need to interrogate further his identity as perceived by others. *Walker's Weekly Penny Journal* was the only contemporary reference to this background, describing, as noted, 'THE TRIAL OF DAVES, a Jew'.[95] By the mid-nineteenth century Jacob was simply assumed to be Jewish. All published accounts described him thus and, without exception, negatively so.[96] Much of this relied on folk memory, which cannot be fully dismissed, especially as it was so persistently and indisputably claimed in this case. In the eighteenth century and beyond, such labelling was common in the courts, the press and everyday discourse, especially in legal cases, no matter whether it described a victim, perpetrator or bystander. A typical example appears in the *Daily Journal* while Jacob Harris was in Horsham gaol. A Mr Bridgett-Jewell Knight decided to advertise to the public the (mis)treatment of his medical condition by a certain Dr Schamberg and how the medication prescribed had made him worse. In the course of the description, Schamberg, in the complainant's increasingly incoherent rant, simply became the 'Jew doctor'.[97] This was, in fact, Meyer Schomberg (1690–1761), one of the most famous medical physicians in England who, in a published attack on London Jewry some twelve years later, showed how 'alienated [he was] from Jewish tradition'.[98]

It *is* just possible that *Walker's Weekly Penny Journal* was adding the description 'Jew' to add spice to the sensation of the case and further stigmatise the perpetrator. On its own, it might be suggested that this source would not be quite enough to confirm his Jewishness, especially as it did not occur elsewhere in the press coverage of his crimes, capture and punishment. Equally, the later memory of Jacob Harris, especially that connected to the Sussex Archaeological Society, could reflect their prejudices, as with the sentences added to the diary of John Stapley by the Reverend Edward Turner confirming not only the murderer's Jewishness but also his occupation as a pedlar. It was his way of dealing with troubling 'matter out of place' and avoiding anomaly and ambiguity.

It is, however, another aspect of the detail in *Walker's Weekly Penny Journal* that adds to the greater certainty that Jacob was indeed Jewish. This was a newspaper that clearly prided itself on extensive coverage of court cases, both past and present. The other newspapers copied each other and either repeated earlier details of Jacob's crimes or simply reported that he had been sentenced to hanging and gibbeting. It is probable that *Walker's Weekly Penny Journal* sent someone to cover the 1734 summer assizes in Horsham and it was there, for the first time, that Jacob's Jewishness emerged in the public realm. Jacob gave his name and pleaded not guilty. It is feasible, following other examples of criminality, that he would have told the presiding judge that he wanted to take his oath on the Bible rather than the New Testament because of his religion. That his Jewishness was not reported earlier by the press came not out of any sensitivity – this was totally lacking in the eighteenth century confrontation with 'the Jew' – but because it was not given in Richard Miles's description of Jacob Harris. Either Miles was not aware of it, or he did not think it was relevant in catching his attacker, relying instead only on his physical appearance and clothing (and keeping in mind that he was struggling to give this description and rewrite his will in his final days and hours).

Moving from the press, the absence of an original printed version of the Ballad makes this a source that does not help us definitively in the search for how Jacob was perceived. The first full printed version in the *Mid-Sussex Times* does describe him as 'This rogue, the Jew, Jacob by name'.[99] As we have seen, however, even if this is taken from a written version, there were variations, and that published five years later by William Albery does not mention Jacob's Jewishness. In Albery's reproduction there were also other small differences from that in the local newspaper. There were competing accounts of Jacob by the interwar period – what would in the early twenty-first century be called 'culture wars'. It is just possible that William Albery, a socialist and internationalist, repressed this negative line about Jacob, especially in the context of the late 1930s – his article appeared just months after the *Kristallnacht* pogrom. To add further support for this interpretation, he had a strong working relationship and close friendship with Lucy Drucker, who was of German Jewish origin, one of many talented medieval palaeographers who were excluded from academia. (Her parents were from Frankfurt – her father was a wine importer – and her sister Amy was an important artist.[109]) Lucy worked freelance for Albery, transcribing documents at the Public Record Office in Chancery Lane.[101]

In contrast, while Gordon Hall was proud to 'say that I have worked with every race in the world' and prided himself on his lack of prejudice towards others, he also told his British Library interviewers that he would not change the words to historic songs, even if 'they caused offence', and thus he would not have avoided referring to Jacob as a Jew.[102] From this, it could be argued that as the Ballad is based largely on contemporary press reporting (which, with the one exception of *Walker's Weekly Penny Journal*, did *not* mention his Jewishness), the original would have followed this example and referenced him only as a 'rogue'. If so, Albery's and then Hall's versions were closer to the original in this respect.

More important, especially if taken in conjunction with *Walker's Weekly Penny Journal*, is Jacob Harris's name/names. It is here, despite his not speaking once in the contemporary archive, that we see his agency through self-naming. It is the use of 'Hirsh' and 'Hirschal' in the legal papers and Sheriff's Cravings that is relevant. They do not prove absolutely that Jacob was Jewish, but they do so, alongside the other evidence – archival and folklore – beyond reasonable doubt.

Until the modern era, Jews had a different tradition of naming from the population around them. In short, Jewish family names did not develop until the early modern era, and unevenly even then. There were some exceptions, but surnames were exceptional, 'used only for outstanding individuals, not for families'.[103] In contrast, family names were generally inheritable in England by the fourteenth century.[104] From the late eighteenth century, new state bureaucracies in central Europe demanded of the Jews that they chose fixed and hereditary surnames.[105] Place and occupation, even house or store signs and personal characteristics, alongside biblical references and repeated first names were how Jews quickly adapted to this new requirement – or more often had these imposed on them. Hirsch (German for deer) or Hirsh (Yiddish for the same animal) was a specifically and exclusively *Jewish* name, relating to the gazelle, the symbol of the tribe of Napthali from the Book of Genesis.[106] Indeed, some German Jews used Hirsch and other such names deliberately rather than the biblical reference from which it came. 'It seemed advisable to a not inconsiderable number to forsake even those surrogate names which might recall the original Hebrew ones: Hirsch (for Napthali), Bendix (for Baruch), Markus (for Mordechai).'[107] Hirsch could also be related to a house sign with a stag or a deer, with examples of this in the German city of Worms.[108]

In English-speaking countries, Hirsh or Hirsch often became anglicised to Hart or Harris, as with our triple murderer. It differed from the same common English surname which was derived from 'Harry'.[109] Taking all the different strands of evidence together, therefore, we must assume with utmost confidence that Jacob/Hirschal Harris/Hirsh was Jewish. That he also went under the first name of James and the old (medieval) English surname of Daves reflected a certain fluidity in how he presented himself to the outside world. It makes him an even more fascinating case for treatment, an embodiment of the 'third space' concept. An intriguing question remains: what was Jacob Harris, of German/continental Jewish origin, doing in Ditchling Common in May 1734?

Part II

# The long eighteenth century

# 3

# Jacob Harris in early modern
# Jewish history

Nations, peoples and religions have rich and wonderful foundation myths. For cities, the most famous is perhaps the creation of Rome and the story of Romulus and Remus. Krakow is not alone in tracing its origins to the defeat of a dragon, while the origins of its Polish neighbour Warsaw rest on the benevolence of an initially hostile mermaid. The ancient port of Southampton settles only slightly more mundanely for the medieval tales of Sir Bevis of Hampton (the town's Norman name) and his squire, the thirty-foot giant Ascupart. The latter was presented in large sixteenth-century paintings at the main gateway to Southampton with 'dark skin and exotic dress', reflecting either African or Middle Eastern origin.[1] And the chivalric romance of Bevis, an influence on Shakespeare's *Hamlet*, was also the inspiration for the first non-religious Yiddish book, *Bovo-Bukh*. First published in 1541, it appealed to the widespread East European Jewish diaspora through the following centuries.[2]

Irrepressibly, the local very quickly becomes the global, blurring, as with Ascupart, the categories of 'majority' and 'minority'. The foundation myth for Brighton Jewry is also transnational and peculiar – possibly unique – in that it is based on the misadventures of a criminal, and triple murderer at that – Jacob Harris. Where Harris 'belongs' in the eighteenth-century Jewish (and non-Jewish) experience – in England and beyond – is at the heart of this chapter. In the process, we will move away from 'majority history' and enter more the inner Jewish world. I will return to a critical question in relation to this study, but one that must remain speculative: what was Jacob doing in rural Sussex, especially as he was the first post-readmission Jew to be there?

The Brighton Jewish community is amongst the oldest of those established outside London after the Jews returned to England. Furthermore, its earliest residents were there from the start of its new life as a Georgian seaside resort when, in the last quarter of the eighteenth century, Brighton, with royal patronage, emerged from its origins as Brighthelmstone, a small fishing village.[3] In 2016, the 250th anniversary of Brighton Jewry was marked by the publication of an 'official' history which provided a timeline starting in 1766. This was the date when the 'first recorded Jewish resident was recorded' – Israel Samuel, a silversmith, 'toyman' and lodging house keeper who lived at the heart of the fast-expanding town.[4] At this point Brighton consisted of only 'seven principal streets … the number of inhabitants being approximately 2,500'.[5] Sixteen years later Emanuel Hyam Cohen arrived from Niederwerrn in Bavaria and the formal religious life of the community began.[6] Even taking the arrival of Samuel as a starting point for Brighton Jewry, this post-dated the hanging and gibbeting of Jacob Harris by some thirty-two years. He was thus living in Sussex decades in advance of its first 'official' Jewish resident, over half a century from the informal creation of a Jewish community and ninety years before the Brighton Hebrew Community was established in 1824. The first purpose-built synagogue opened in 1838 – the erection of this Jewish space was thus opened a century *after* Jacob's gibbeting.[7]

Despite these alternative narratives of 'pioneer Jews', in earlier histories of Brighton Jewry and in more popular heritage work Jacob Harris is still represented as the founding father of the community. This was especially so as his very existence developed a mythic quality, having an appeal beyond more mundane searching for roots. Having mentioned Samuel as 'the first recorded Jew in Brighton' in a 1968 lecture to the Jewish Historical Society of England, David Spector corrected himself by adding that 'There is, however, a *local legend* of Jacob Harris – a Jewish pedlar – who in the year 1734 committed murder at the Royal Oak, Ditchling, near Brighton [it is eight miles due north], was hung at Horsham, and his corpse suspended for many years from a gibbet outside the Royal Oak [my emphasis].'[8] At a popular level, Jacob's early presence in Sussex proved important for later Jews in the county establishing a sense of place. Yehuda Efune, brought up around Brighton, as a teenager and an aspiring writer was inspired by visiting the Ditchling Museum and learning about the Jewish triple murderer. Now rabbi of the Chelsea synagogue, he recalled also the talented but eccentric Brighton correspondent of the *Jewish Chronicle*, who claimed to have taken a photograph of the ghost of Jacob Harris (though she had also maintained that she had captured images of UFOs!).[9]

That it was thought Jacob might only have existed as a folk tale indicates the limited academic engagement with him – Jacob Harris's memory existed largely outside 'history'. While there were many historical studies of British Jews published from the 1730s onwards, the only mention of Jacob was in a whimsical note by Cecil Roth in the *Jewish Chronicle* in 1936 concerning 'Jewish Place-Names'. Roth was the most prominent twentieth-century historian of British Jewry until his death in 1970.[10] In 'Jewish Place-Names', he preceded Spector in being tentative about the story, commenting that Jacob's Post was 'said to have been so named in honour of one Jacob Harris, who met a suspensory death on a gibbet there in 1734'.[11] Roth's papers show him to be a devotee of Jewish references in *Notes and Queries*, and it was perhaps through this factually obsessed source that he became aware of the murders, even then being cautious about repeating the story as fact. Roth never referenced him again, even in his articles on Jewish pedlars.[12]

Some eighty years after Roth's aside about the site in Ditchling Common, Marcus Roberts, in a popular internet Anglo-Jewish heritage 'trail', provided a set of 'key dates' for Brighton and Hove, which were heavily reliant on Spector's first contribution to the subject. Roberts also began his trail at 1734 and gave Jacob the honour of being the first Jew in (or near) the town. Curiously, considering the amount of popular writing on these murders by the twenty-first century, much by then available through the internet, there is still a degree of uncertainty present in this narrative: 'Jacob Harris is *reputed* to have committed a murder [sic] at Ditchling near Brighton [my emphasis].'[13] Whether Roberts's doubt is about Jacob's very existence, or his guilt, is unclear. Fourteen years after his 1968 lecture, and more confident in his research, David Spector published a survey history of 'Jewry in Sussex'. He now included material about the medieval Jewish communities in the important religious and commercial centres of Chichester, Arundel and Lewes, including accusations made against them of ritual murder.[14]

Alongside his more extensive time span, Spector was now more assertive about our anti-hero. He highlighted that from the expulsion in 1290 'there is a gap until the early part of the eighteenth century when the first reference is to the fate of an itinerant Jewish pedlar named Jacob Harris, hanged for murder on 31 August 1734'. Even then, Spector still saw Emanuel Cohen as 'the real founder of the Brighton community', presumably as it was from him that sustained religious practice in the town originated. There is no evidence of Jacob Harris's religiosity, though his flagrant disregard of the sixth commandment suggests he might not have been a very pious Jew.[15]

Spector's pioneer research on Brighton was crucial in providing a framework for later research to flourish, including being the first to bring Jacob Harris into Jewish historiography beyond Cecil Roth's throwaway sentence in the 1930s. Nevertheless, some of Spector's assumptions regarding Harris need to be

questioned: that he was definitively a pedlar, was itinerant – and most significantly that he should be viewed as an outsider to the Jewish world because his
'contribution' was not religious. Yet the problem of the 'archive' remains, especially the small amount of material that has survived from the early eighteenth
century. And while contemporary Jewish sources will come more to the fore in
this chapter, they still reflect wealth and power in the community – those of the
poor and marginal are rarely heard. When they are, it is more often through
distorted legal discourse or as a 'problem' to be dealt with by elite Jews. In both
communal records and those of the judiciary, the Jewish lower classes were
presented as a problem. But the task to create a Jewish history from below for
the eighteenth century is not impossible. It is simply necessary to regard the
surviving archive as both friend and foe.

## Early readmission Anglo-Jewish history and Jacob Harris

Organisationally and in terms of population, there is no doubt that London
has been the dominant place of Jewish settlement since Oliver Cromwell read-
mitted the Jews to England in the 1650s. Anglo-Jewish historical writing not
only confirms but also tends to overstate the influence of London at the cost of
neglecting the provinces. As Cecil Roth noted in 1950: 'the historiography of
the Jews in England has hitherto shewn little interest in what went on outside
the capital'.[16] There is an assumption still lurking that for 'England – even
Britain – read London', and as a result, a self-perpetuating bias in the secondary
literature. Bill Williams, whose *The Making of Manchester Jewry* (1976) managed
to break free from London-centrism, is in a class of its own in such local studies
with regard to the quality of its research, contextualisation and style. Tellingly,
he remarked that when he started off writing it, 'It took me some time to rec-
ognise just how large and historically important the Jewish community [there]
was.'[17]

Cecil Roth's *The Rise of Provincial Jewry* only provided a sketch map, albeit
an extremely useful one – especially with regard to the importance of pedlars
in building up nascent communities. Roth, writing in defensive mode, insisted
that Jews were to be found in *all* parts of Britain and not just in areas of urban
concentration, as anti-alien campaigners prejudicially asserted. Reflecting the
ongoing insecurities of the Jewish world during and after the Second World
War, Roth emphasised that it was 'not only of interest, *but of importance*, to dem-
onstrate that the English Jews are rooted in this country – in fact, that their
history in one provincial county after the other, far from being a development

of the last couple of generations, goes back for … many centuries [my empha-sis]'.[18] The gaps – with the exception of Williams on Manchester – have been covered unevenly subsequent to Roth's brief intervention.

It is true (except for the medieval period, when only one fifth of the Jewish population were in London) that around 70 per cent of British Jewry lived, and continue to live, in the capital and its suburbs. For the first few dec-ades after readmission London totally dominated, and within that city, set-tlements immediately to the east, which were free from the restrictions within its boundaries, were where almost all the Jews were located. Slowly, how-ever, especially through peddling and other trading, there were incursions into wider geographies, both physical and in the imaginary. From the mid-eighteenth century onwards, the first sizeable provincial communities were to be found in ports such as Plymouth, Portsmouth, Exeter, Penzance, Falmouth, Bristol, Chatham, King's Lynn and Liverpool. These were numerically much larger than communities in the new industrial conurbations of Manchester and Birmingham, which took well into the Victorian era to rival and then overtake them demographically, followed by Leeds and Glasgow.

The pattern, especially in seaports well away from London, was for Jewish pedlars to begin to congregate, perhaps by the 1740s in a linked chain of lodg-ing houses 'in which Jewish travellers were familiar and which could be used as steppingstones in long provincial journeys'. Alternatively, 'Groups of pedlars who surrounded more populated areas congregated in … inns on a Friday night, stayed over Saturday [for the Sabbath], and set out again on Sunday evening.'[19] More successful itinerant Jews might accumulate enough capital to rent small shops, and from such enterprise came permanent settlement and the early provincial communities outlined. This model is too tidy and does not allow for settlements that proved to be unsustainable even in the short term. It also ignores the fact that many Jewish pedlars did *not* advance into the shop-keeping classes, and led lives of continued poverty and insecurity. Some simply perished on the road. How then does Jacob Harris conform within this model of almost inevitable progress – what Cecil Roth impishly called the 'Antecedents of Aristocracy'?[20]

In his study of magic and the legacy of slavery in Madagascar, anthro-pologist David Graeber emphasises that 'A culture isn't "about" anything. It's about everything. People don't live their lives to prove some academic's point.'[21] The Victorian antiquarians put Jacob Harris in a box labelled 'Jew pedlar' *not* through any deep understanding of the dynamics of British Jewish social and economic history and the limited opportunities available in the first centuries following readmission, but because he, or rather their construction of him, fitted their expectations of what such an outsider would be and how they would behave (that is, *very* badly). Their grim determination that this was the occupation (and nature) of Jacob Harris has blinkered others to believe it was definitively the case – well beyond the mid-Victorian era. This even included David Spector, whose quest to 'find' Jacob Harris predated this author's study by close to half a century.

Inserted in the Stapley diaries with the relevant entries about the murders are Spector's notes. He wanted to get close to the evidence yet did not seem to grasp, even when faced with the original manuscript, that the description of Jacob Harris as a 'Jew pedlar' was purely an invention of the Reverend Turner.[22] This was a case of an absence in plain sight. There was equally no mention of Jacob as a pedlar in the coroner's report which David Spector had transcribed – as noted, he was given the standard legal description of 'labourer' – or in any of the numerous newspaper references to the murders, the trials, the hanging and the gibbeting.[23]

Nevertheless, given the pattern of settlement that has been outlined so far, it would make perfect sense for Jacob Harris to have been a Jewish pedlar who had expanded his trade beyond London – or at least to begin with. Keeping Graeber's advice in mind, however, we need to be careful not to put him in this category just yet. More broadly, just because the evidence is almost unequivocal that he was indeed of Jewish origin, it does not follow that this was his *dominant* identity. Just as Jacob's Post functioned as a 'third space', Jacob himself may well have regarded himself beyond the binaries of 'Jewish' and 'non-Jewish' – if he thought about such matters at all. And while it is almost certain that he would have either been born or grown up in London, it seems that he had, by the 1730s, established strong roots in Sussex as part of a smuggling community. The county was ideally suited for illicit trading: 'Its long coastline was not heavily populated … and it was both near London and yet remote, because of the notoriously muddy and dark Sussex lanes.' Tea, especially, was a high-value commodity, and as much as three-quarters of it was 'illegally' imported during the 1730s and 1740s. If Jacob had links to the criminal fraternity in London, such connections would have been of great value in selling on smuggled products such tea and brandy to be sold to a ready market in the capital city through underworld 'agents'.[24]

In Sussex there was not yet a supporting network of lodging houses or inns where Jews congregated, but Jacob Harris, while perhaps maintaining links to 'Jewish' London, was now also part of a different criminal community. It may

and Portuguese community took legal action against Osborne. It was a case that revealed both the strength and the limitations of antisemitism in Britain. The publication was entitled 'A true and surprising Relation of a Murder and Cruelty that was committed by the Jews lately arrived from *Portugal*'. It claimed that in February 1732 these Jews 'had burnt a Woman and new born Infant … because the Infant was begotten by a Christian'. The author clearly had medieval ritual murder in mind, as he claimed that such cruelty and murder committed by the Jews was outlawed by ancient royal decree in England. The problem in prosecuting for libel was that no individuals were specifically mentioned by Osborne as the murderers. The further argument was then used that the pamphlet had induced a 'Breach of the Peace, in inciting a Mob to the destruction of a whole set of People' and that it would be 'pernicious to suffer such scandalous Reflections to go unpunished'. The court decided that because the publication 'had so much incensed the Mob against the Jews, that they had assaulted and beat in a most outrageous Manner, the Prosecutor, who was a Jew', it should be suppressed.[32] A newspaper report of the case was a little more circumspect on these attacks, stating that as a result of Osborne's accusations the Jews 'were frequently insulted by the Populace', but not referencing physical attacks.[33]

The case was serious enough to merit the attention of the President of Bevis Marks, Jacob Israel Suavo. His committee 'resolved to proceed with all force and whatever expenses are required or paid in advance'.[34] While it is possible that the violence was overstated to win the legal case, from 1736 through to 1738 the synagogue paid a substantial sum to the 'City Marshal [and] Condestables' 'for keeping the rabble quiet'.[35] This threat was thus taken seriously by the leaders of the Jewish community, and a revival of the medieval blood libel shows that there was a strong residue of antipathy in British culture of an unreconstructed nature – confirmed two decades later in the 'Jew Bill' controversy. Indeed, there may well be a linkage here and it is possible that Osborne had wider goals. It has been suggested that his campaign could have been 'a counter stroke in return for the efforts of the Jews to gain an enlargement of their rights: in 1730, for example, they had … sent a petition to the City authorities asking for an increase in the number of sworn Jewish brokers'.[36] The court found in favour of Suavo and that the forces of law and order could be marshalled to protect the Jews – albeit requested by themselves and at a sizeable price. This was, however, standard law enforcement practice before the creation of the Bow Street Runners.

However vile Osborne's pamphlet was, and the ensuing atmosphere of fear that was created, it did not lead to anything approximating a pogrom or even

life-threatening injuries. The distance from the capital and the lack of prominence given to Jacob Harris's Jewishness meant that his murders did not come
to the attention of the Jewish elders of London.[37] Yet rather than an imagined
crime, as with that alleged by Osborne, this was real and bloody, and involved if
not a child, then two defenceless women. A more violently antisemitic-minded
culture would have made more of Jacob Harris and even the hint of Jewish
involvement in these three murders. Nor would it have allowed him subsequently to become a local folk hero. And however much tension and hooligan-
ism Osborne's libel caused, it did not form the basis of a showcase trial such
as that of Joseph Oppenheimer ('Jew Suss') in Germany during the later 1730s
when, as noted, this 'court Jew' was eventually hanged and gibbeted in 1738
without any specific charges against him.[38]

In London in 1732, the judgment essentially suppressed Osborne to protect
the well-being of the Jewish community. The trial of Jacob Harris in Horsham
during the summer of 1734 was incredibly brief by later standards, but he was
found guilty according to the evidence against him and following eighteenth-
century legal norms in England. Jacob's Jewishness was not a factor in the decision to hang and gibbet him. Statistically, while by the middle of the eighteenth
century 'the percentage of Jews sentenced to death was higher than their relative share in the population', this largely reflected the trades they occupied and
recent trends in Jewish criminality, rather than necessarily any direct bias in the
courts.[39] In contrast, the Oppenheimer case was so prominent in the history of
Jewish/non-Jewish relations that it became the foundation for later attacks on
the Jews in Germany.

It remains that the fear of the Jewish leadership in early Georgian England
was that there was enough violence, exclusion and prejudice articulated pub-
licly in print and speech at home to merit genuine concern. Moreover, despite
the limitations compared to the continent, this did not mean things could not
change for the worse. Policing crime and poverty were thus ways that the position of English Jews could be protected.

While England provided greater safety, stability and status to Jews, it still
shared a literary and popular culture that regarded the Jews as dangerous and
other, even if this was slowly being contested by a more tolerant approach.
Large sections of the press were extremely hostile to the 'Jew Bill', and a pamphlet campaign added to the heated opposition. More reasoned and eloquent
than many was the 107-page objection to the 'Jew Bill' from 'A Merchant' – the
pseudonym reflects the fact that city financiers were one of the groups most
critical of this legislation, fearing direct competition. Penned by the merchant,

philanthropist (he was Governor of the Foundling Hospital), opponent of tea drinking and proponent of men's use of umbrellas, Jonas Hanway, it was just one of many of his publications, but clearly a cause that he was deeply committed to. Predicting Enoch Powell over two hundred years later on the subject of New Commonwealth migration, Hanway argued against the '*mistaken notion that a Jew born here is a natural-born Englishman*'.[40]

For Powell, the reasons that West Indians and Asians, even when born here, could not become 'Englishmen' was for reasons of culture (he denied, totally unconvincingly, that it was about 'race').[41] Hanway argued that 'the Jews ... are not entitled to naturalization for two plain reasons: the first is because they are Jews; the second because they are not Christians'.[42] There is a subtle distinction here which takes Hanway closer to Powell. There was something inherent in Jewish character that Hanway believed was immutable. This comes out clearly in the economic and social threat he believed Jews posed to England, and was most blatant in the occupations they occupied. This takes us back to the case of Jacob Harris.

The number of useful Jews, argued Hanway, was miniscule and could easily be dismissed. Much more important and dangerous were a 'Train of *hawkers*, and *pedlars*, and *traffickers in every imaginable* commodity, in every *imaginable* way, but very few in *that* which is deemed *regular*, *honorable*, and according to the ordinary rules of civil polity.' Hanway continued that 'In this general list, we must include those who buy, and sell stolen goods.' These traders made up the large majority of the Jews, Hanway argued, and even if the richer Jews helped maintain them, this did not diminish the damage done by both, and especially the '*poor* [who were] really a *burden* to a nation'.[43]

Although his criminalisation and belittling of Jewish pedlars and the like was severely prejudiced, Hanway did in his distorted way outline the economic marginality and hence occupational fluidity of many poorer Jews in Georgian England. Jacob Harris may well have been an extreme version of the tendencies which Hanway identified in his polemic. Similarly, the author's querying of the relationship between the 'necessitous' and the 'opulent' Jews needs teasing out further in relation to the early organisational structures and tensions within the Jewish community/communities of England.[44]

The first to be officially allowed back, indeed encouraged by Cromwell to come to England from the 1650s onwards, were largely elite Sephardi traders from Holland and the Dutch colonies, where they had firmly established global family mercantile networks as 'port Jews'. Initially the position of these pioneer English Jews was still quite precarious, both in law and in relation to religious and economic opposition to them. This, however, slowly eased, especially when William of Orange became king in 1688. William had already recognised the economic worth of the Sephardi merchants and the wealth they created for Holland through international trading.[45] And, more from a position of religious tolerance, the Irish philosopher John Toland as early as 1714 argued in favour of Jews being treated equally and with full rights in the British Isles:

> far from being an Excrescence or Spunge (as some wou'd have it) and a useless member in the Commonwealth, or being ill subjects, and a dangerous people on any account, that they are as obedient, peaceable, useful, and advantageous as any; and even more so than many others.[46]

Toland was aware that others would highlight their faults, and he acknowledged that 'There are among the *Jews*, to be sure, sordid wretches, sharpers, extortioners, villains of all sorts and degrees.' He retorted, however: 'where is that happy nation, where is that religious profession, of which the same may not be as truly affirm'd?'[47] Even if the status of the Jews gradually became less tentative, the 'Jew Bill' controversy revealed that the tensions over Jews being allowed back to England in the 1650s still lingered close to a century later. Their alleged criminal nature, especially linked to trading, remained at the heart of the discussion. The 'Jew Bill' was, as Robert Liberles argues, the 'first real opportunity since Readmission for a public debate in England on the status of the Jews'.[48] Toland's rational and tolerant approach remained well ahead of its time, as was his belief that history proved that nations suffered economically when Jews were persecuted or removed.[49]

For the first decades after readmission, the Sephardim were numerically the largest group of Jews in England, though their numbers were still small. In 1695, there were just 495 Sephardim linked to the synagogue.[50] In that year a census was carried out in London from which roughly 850 Jews have been identified. Nearly half were in just two parishes to the east of the city, St James Duke's Place and St Katherine Creechurch, consisting of around 185 families. Less than a quarter, or just over 200, were Ashkenazi Jews, who were mainly poor and well over half of whom were of German origin.[51] Amongst their ranks, however, were some wealthy merchants from Hamburg whose trading networks and success matched those of the Sephardi port Jews. Most prominent was Benjamin Levy, high up in the East India Company and the Royal African Company, both heavily involved with the slave trade.[52] Levy was thus a contemporary of the now notorious Edward Colston in the Royal African Company, in which the Bristol slave trader was deputy governor.[53]